W9-AYS-144

DEEP ROOTS

THOMASTON PUBLIC LIBRARY
THOMASTON, MAINE

Bluehill, Me.

402594

Courtesy of Robert Sweetall

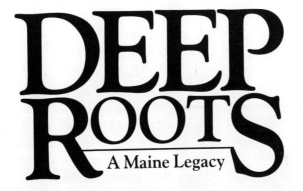

DEEP ROOTS

A Maine Legacy

BY ESTHER WOOD

THOMASTON PUBLIC LIBRARY
THOMASTON, MAINE

YANKEE BOOKS

CAMDEN, MAINE

974.1
Woo

© 1990 by Esther Wood

No part of this book may be reproduced or transmitted in any
form or by any means, electronic or mechanical, including
photocopying, recording, or by any information storage and
retrieval system, without the written permission of the
publisher, except by a reviewer quoting brief passages in a
magazine, newspaper or broadcast. Address inquiries to
Yankee Books, 62 Bay View Street, Camden, Maine 04843.

Cover design by Lurelle Cheverie
Text design by Peter Tibbetts

Printed in the United States of America

Library of Congress Cataloging-in-Publication Data

Wood, Esther.
    Deep roots.

    1. Blue Hill (Me.)—History.   I. Title.
F29.B78W66   1989   974.1'45   89-25011
ISBN 0–912769–44–0

Second Printing, 1990

*To Audway and Phyllis Treworgy
with gratitude*

Contents

FIRST SETTLERS AND SONS

GENERATION TO GENERATION

Courtesy of J. M. Hinckley

Author's Preface

This book is not a history of Blue Hill. It is a collection of essays, biographical sketches, and reminiscences. A few of the pieces appeared earlier in *Down East Magazine, Maine Life,* and the *Ellsworth American.*

There are persons and families who might well have been included. My choices were determined by the amount of material available.

The accepted spelling for my native town is Blue Hill. That is the spelling that I have used, except in cases of quotations.

I am grateful to the people who have helped me. James Russell Wiggins encouraged me to undertake the writing of the book. Teresa Slaven has been my typist. Many friends have answered my questions, shared their recollections, given me information, and made corrections. Elizabeth Wescott, Jerry Long, Gay Wojtowicz, and Betty Bates have loaned me material. Ellen Bates allowed me the use of many of Roland Howard's papers. Wallace Hinckley loaned me the diaries of Augustus Hinckley. The librarians at the Blue Hill Public Library have also aided me. Robert Sweetall loaned his cards to be used as illustrations. Jerold Hinckley allowed his old photographs to be used.

My historical material has been taken from a variety of sources, such as *Journals of Jonathan Fisher*; R. G. F. Candage's *Historical Sketches of Blue Hill, Maine* (1907); Williamson's *History of Maine, 1614–1833* (1832); Otis Littlefield's *Autobiography* (unpublished); the scrapbooks made by Josie Snow Barker; William Hinckley's articles published in the *Weekly Packet*; the papers of Roland Howard; genealogical sketches by Byron Darling; a scrapbook made by Effie Kline; Rowe's *Maritime History of Maine* (1948); records of the Blue Hill Baptist Church; the records of the town of Blue Hill; files of the *Ellsworth American*; journals of Augustus Hinckley; the 1907 *Historical Address* by James Long; the records of the James A. Garfield Post of the American Legion; the *Perry-Long Genealogy* by Elwell H. Perr; and *A Biography of Architects in Maine:*, published by the Maine Historic Preservation Commission.

I am a descendant of six of the founding families of Blue Hill. This book is my tribute to the town of my ancestors.

Born and Bred

Village Landing, Bluehill, Me.

Courtesy of Robert Sweetall

1

Native Sailors

IN MY CHILDHOOD I saw reminders of my grandfather Wood's years at sea. In my bedroom was his hardwood sea chest, its rope handles held in place by pieces of mahogany, wood out of company with the native pine. In the kitchen was his captain's chair, made of pine and bearing scars of its years aboard vessels. Behind the door in Uncle Arthur's dining room was the captain's spyglass. In Uncle's kitchen was Grandfather's dough table, a square homemade table with two deep drawers and a flat top that was edged by a high rim on three sides. The rim was added to keep dishes from sliding off when the vessel was in rough seas. Aunt Nellie used the tabletop as a flour board. She often re-marked, "Likely this dough table has seen more years of use aship than it will ever see ashore." Both my father and uncle liked to talk about the years when their father went to sea. They taught me how important the sea once was to Blue Hill.

It was by sea that the first settlers came to Blue Hill. It was by sea that their descendants for four generations sent out lumber and produce, granite and ore, fish and potash, cattle and hides, and brought in sugar and molasses, coffee, tea, vinegar, and rum. In later days, groceries, canned goods, kerosene, and coal came by sea. It was by sea that people went to Rockland, Portland, Salem, and Boston. The sea opened for them a wider world than the one bounded by the Salt Pond, the freshwater ponds, Blue Hill Mountain, and McHard's Stream.

The first settlers were pioneers. They cut the trees and cleared the land and built houses and barns. They planted gardens, hunted, and fished in nearby waters.

Congress in Washington's administration encouraged coastal farmers to fish. Congress passed a law that provided a bounty for pickled cod and dried cod. A little later the bounty was changed to a flat rate paid each fishing boat: $1.50 per ton for smaller craft, $2.50 for larger ones. Three-eighths of the money went to the captain and the remainder was divided among the crew. It was required that a vessel fish for at least four months a year.

There were critics of government aid to the fishermen. Elder James Gilpatrick of Blue Hill's Baptist Church was one of them. One day he criticized the bounty at the Wood dinner table. Without laying down knife and fork, Captain Wood answered him: "Well, Elder Gilpatrick, I notice that you accept bounty money in the contribution box."

The federal bounty brought prosperity to coastal Maine. By the mid-1820s Maine owned a fifth of the United States tonnage engaged in fishing, employed 2,600 men as fishermen, and included within its borders half of all the fishing establishments on the Atlantic seaboard. Sometimes a local merchant in a coastal village furnished the vessel and the outfit. The captain and the crew all fished on shares and no one received any salary except the cook, who was paid monthly wages. Blue Hill fishing vessels went to Castine to buy salt to preserve their catch. One Blue Hill ship engaged in the trade of bringing salt from Spain to Castine. The first Blue Hill fishermen fished in sight of the mountain, but later they fished out of sight of land. In the late nineteenth century some of them went to Rockland or Bucksport and signed on large vessels that fished on the Grand Banks.

Some Blue Hill men fished but did not go to sea. They were farmers who built weirs across the narrow coves of their saltwater fields and in August caught porgies (menhaden). They boiled the fish in great kettles set over blazing fires on the beach. They pressed the oil from the cooked fish and poured it into barrels that were later sold to a dealer from Rockland. The oil was used to make paint. Farmers fertilized their fields with the fish chum. Prosperity from the sale of porgies was short-lived. In 1878 the porgies suddenly deserted the Maine coast.

Trade with the West Indies was important to Blue Hill sailors. My father, born in 1866, knew the details of the trade because for several decades his father went to the Caribbean Islands. Captain Giles Wood made two trips a year to the Caribbean, with Port au Prince or Havana the usual ports of call. He left Maine in late December and with luck reached the islands in three weeks. He took on a return cargo and was home by February. He reloaded and made a second voyage that was usually completed by April. The ship was laid up in the summer months, the season for hurricanes and yellow fever in the Caribbean. In the summer the captain gardened and put his vessel in shape for another season of trade. In the fall he sometimes took kiln wood to Rockland or cordwood to Portland.

Captain Wood took to the West Indies lumber, staves, hoops, and "ventures." The "ventures" were produce raised on the farm or articles made in home workshops. He took apples, potatoes, beets, and carrots. He took baskets and wooden ware and homespun cloth. Grandmother Friend sent round cheeses, some of them seasoned with sage. His cargo on the way back was mainly molasses for the Brown Company in Portland. In the mid-nineteenth century Brown owned the second largest sugarhouse in the United States. Earlier, Maine sea captains had imported West Indies rum, but by 1840 it was cheaper to buy West Indies molasses and have Maine distilleries make the rum.

Some years Captain Wood made only one trip to the Caribbean. Instead of a second trip to Cuba or Haiti, he made two trips to Charleston. He took down lumber and brought back raw cotton for the Brunswick mills. Likely he brought some for George Stevens's Blue Hill mill.

My father, as a small child, used to pray that "Pa Giles" would bring "Johnny" candy and chocolate and guava jelly. His prayers were always answered.

The vessels that engaged in the West Indies trade were small craft, usually with a crew of four or five. Sometimes they took along Blue Hill coopers who stayed in Cuba for a few months to assemble barrels and boxes. The Harpswell storyteller, Elijah Kellogg, wrote children's novels that give a fine description of the trade with the islands of the Caribbean. Stores that sold products from the Caribbean bore signs that announced "W.I. GOODS." I recall seeing one such sign on the front of a long-closed store. The store was in western Maine, possibly in Eliot or Harpswell.

Blue Hill sailors also sailed on great three-masted schooners that carried lumber. Some were Blue Hill–built; some were not. But wherever the vessel was built, the crew used the same vocabulary to describe the cargo:

Deals: pieces of timber to be sawed when they reached their destination.

Long lumber: planks and boards.

Short lumber: clapboards, laths, fence posts, and shingles.

The lumber vessels also carried knees (roots) of juniper and hemlock, masts of pine and spruce, and hemlock bark for tanning. After railroads came, they carried cedar sleepers and posts. Lumber ships sailed to England; Mediterranean, Atlantic, and South American ports; and to Texas and California.

Maine-built vessels took lime to market from the kilns of Rockland, Rockport, and Camden. As early as 1835 those three towns were producing 750,000 casks of lime yearly. I do not know that Blue Hill vessels took lime to market. Lime was a dangerous cargo to carry. If the lime became wet it caused a fire. I do know that many local boats were "wooders." William Rowe, in his book *The Maritime History of Maine*, wrote that in the 1850s over 500 sloops, schooners,

Bluehill Bay from The Homestead, Bluehill, Maine.

Courtesy of Robert Sweetall

and brigs were taking kiln wood to the towns on Penobscot Bay. They took cordwood and "shooks," waste from sawmills, often gathered from the water of the Penobscot River or from harbors where there were sawmills.

Blue Hillers may have gone on vessels that took Brooksville ice to the cities. They certainly sailed on the granite-carriers. I saw three such craft in my childhood and young womanhood:

Lois M. Candage, a schooner built in East Blue Hill and owned by Captain George Candage.

Annie and Reuben, a schooner that had a reputation for speed. The *Annie and Reuben* was specially built to carry granite. Her masts were spaced well apart in order to facilitate the loading of stone through a large hatch amidships. As late as the 1930s she was taking Stonington granite to New York.

The Herald of the Morning, a three-master as beautiful as her name. Before 1916 she came to the Chase Granite Company for granite.

Blue Hill sailors started their seafaring career by "bounty fishing." The vessel never went far out to sea. It cruised among the islands, going into a harbor at night. On Sundays they went to Outer Long Island or Swan's Island, where the men went ashore.

The next step was "going coasting." A boy or young man signed up to go on a vessel that went from port to port delivering and taking on goods. Portland was a favorite port of call. There, the men went ashore to play ball on Munjoy Hill and see the sights on Congress Street. Coasting was a good way to learn geography. It was a good way to work up from hand to second mate, from second mate to first mate, and perhaps even to become the captain. Sometimes an empty vessel could not find another cargo and the sailors were discharged. They had to go to a sailors' boardinghouse while they searched for a new berth. R. G. F. Candage, a Blue Hill sailor, was once away from home for nine years while he shifted from one vessel to another. Candage was one of the fortunate ones who went from hand to captain. He achieved the sailor's dream of becoming the captain of a full-rigged ship that engaged in the China trade.

Blue Hill sailors knew the ports of the Atlantic seaboard and the Caribbean as well as they knew Castine andBucksport and Ellsworth. Some of them knew faraway places. Sewall Snowman knew Montevideo, Egypt, and Liverpool. Thomas Osgood knew Brazil and the Crimean Peninsula. Addison Webber went to the Persian Gulf, Africa, China, and the East Indies. R. G. F. Candage went to San Francisco, Hawaii, Hong Kong, Melbourne, Adelaide, Bombay, Calcutta, London, Le Havre, and Liverpool.

Blue Hill men were sometimes shipwrecked. Dr. Otis Littlefield of Blue Hill made a list of thirty Blue Hill–built ships that were lost between 1833 and 1875. Blue Hill vessels suffered a variety of misfortunes: "wrecked," "struck a ledge," "thrown on her beam-ends," "foundered," "never heard of again," "her end unknown," "collision at sea," "went ashore high and dry," "struck upon a bar," "caught in a hurricane and never heard from thereafter," "went ashore in a dense fog," "her chains parted in a northeast gale and snowstorm," "dismasted in a hurricane," "wrecked off Cape Cod in a gale," "was struck by a high sea, hove down, masts went by the board," "thrown on her beam-end and abandoned," and "burned by the Confederates."

R. G. F. Candage, in his *Historical Sketches of Blue Hill* (1905), listed the families from the Sedgwick line to the Head-of-the-Bay. Mr. Candage, as a retired sea captain, took great care to note those who were sailors. His father was James Candage. He and his wife had seven sons who were sailors. Six of the seven were lost at sea or died of disease in a foreign port. Mrs. Candage's first husband was Captain William Walker. He and a son were both lost at sea. Numerous members of several Clough families were sailors. Some of them were unlucky. Ashman and Robert Bruce were lost at sea; Cheever died in Peru; Rufus drowned when he fell through a hole in a San Francisco wharf. Most Blue Hill families in the nineteenth century had a son or two who went to sea.

John Warren Kane was Surry-born but he became a Blue Hill resident. He was one of the town's last captains. He went to sea in the early decades of the twentieth century. His spicy personality and quick humor made him a loved and much-quoted citizen. I recall that my father used to quote him on the subject of adult-child relationships: "Correct one of those children for tracking mud into my house! Never! I'd rather have every man in town down on me than win the enmity of one of those young ones." Captain Kane once rescued English citizens from a sinking ship. To the delight of his fellow townsmen, Queen Victoria gave him an award and a silver cup.

In the twentieth century, Maurice Howard, a Horton descendant, became the captain of the *Alexander Hamilton*, owned by the Day Line. This steamship was a Hudson River boat that ran between New York City and Albany.

The sea changed Blue Hill sailors. They were different from their fathers and sons who stayed at home. They were more tolerant and less bound by tradition. They knew the wonders of the deep and the strangeness of faraway places.

2

Native Storekeepers

IN THE SECOND DECADE of the twentieth century there were six grocery stores in Blue Hill. There was a store at South Blue Hill, one at Blue Hill Falls, two at the Head-of-the-Bay, one at North Blue Hill, and one at East Blue Hill. There were similarities among them. Four of them were near the waters of the bay. Several were associated with certain families: The one at East Blue Hill with the Longs; Twining's store with the Parker Family; Merrill and Hinckley's with the Hinckleys; the one at the Falls with the Conary Family; and the one at South Blue Hill with the Sylvesters.

Several of the stores had a lodge association. Twining's store occupied the first floor of the Odd Fellows building. The store at East Blue Hill was in a building owned by the Grange. The Daughters of Liberty and Master Mechanics met on the third floor of the Merrill and Hinckley building. All of the stores had chairs for loafers and customers who came to the store to tell and hear news and to buy groceries.

Some of the stores had distinctive features. The store at East Blue Hill was for a time owned by the Grange. In front of Twining's store were the town scales, so large that a load of hay or wood or coal could be driven on them to be weighed. The stores at the Falls and South Blue Hill contained rooms that served as post offices. The latter handled the mail for the post office on Long Island, called Seaville. Islanders picked up the Long Island mail every weekday in the summer months. Merrill and Hinckley's store occupied two floors and sold goods not carried by the others: clothing, furniture, dishes, clocks, rugs, and farm tools. The Merrill and Hinckley store was heated by a large furnace rather than by center stoves.

Goods for all the stores came by steamboat and were unloaded at the wharves in South Blue Hill and on Peters's Point in the village. Previously, in the 1890s, the steamboat called at a wharf in East Blue Hill. In winters when the inner bay froze over, goods were unloaded at the South Blue Hill wharf. In winters when the outer bay was ice-sealed, goods came by train to Ellsworth and were hauled over snow-covered roads to Blue Hill. Storekeepers ordered goods from "drummers," salesmen who went from store to store. The men usually came to town by steamboat, took a room at a local boardinghouse, and spent several days making the circuit of Blue Hill, Brooklin, and Sedgwick by horse-drawn buggy or sleigh.

Customers usually bought goods on credit. Each family had a storebook in which were listed the weekly purchases. At the end of each month, a customer "paid up." At the stores a man could buy staple groceries, kerosene, tobacco, candy, thread, cloth, and grain for farm animals. There were a few canned goods: corn, beans, peas, salmon, and sardines. Most of the stores sold cookies, fig bars, Mary Janes (large molasses cookies), and coconut bars. Some farmers brought in potatoes, turnips, beets, carrots, pumpkins, and squash. Butter and eggs were the most common exchange items. A customer was given credit for the goods sold to the store.

The two stores at the village, the store at South Blue Hill, and the one at East Blue Hill delivered groceries and grain. At first they used horse-drawn vehicles and then small trucks. When the storekeeper delivered groceries, he took orders for the next delivery.

The twenties and thirties brought great changes to Blue Hill storekeeping. By 1920, the village had a third grocery store when Ernest McIntyre began to sell groceries in his meat market. The storebook system was displaced by the slip-charge account system. The telephone led to the grad-

Courtesy of J. M. Hinckley

ual retirement of "drummers." When the steamboats no longer came to Blue Hill, goods came to town by way of Ellsworth and the trains. By the close of the 1920s, most stores had gas tanks out front. As more and more customers bought Model Ts, delivery of goods was less frequent.

In the late 1920s, stores started to sell bread. It is probable that Sherman Hinckley was the first to sell bread, Hinckley-made. He sold bread in the same store where his wife sold gifts and ice cream and he had a photography shop. For a time some grocers bought bread from the local baker, Linwood Leighton. Mrs. Carrie Conary made the first bread that the Grange store sold. In a few years all the stores were buying bread from the Hathaway Company in Bangor. The store at South Blue Hill bought Huston cookies, made in Boston.

By the late 1920s there was greater variety in canned goods. Canned pineapple kindled a craze for pineapple pies, and tinned oysters started the custom of serving oyster stews at lodge suppers. Deviled ham relieved the monotony of egg sandwiches. Orange marmalade supplemented Mother's jellies.

The first grocery store that I knew was the one owned by Merrill and Hinckley. The name of the store always raised questions. The owners were Merrill Hinckley and Frank Merrill. The men were cousins who had married sisters. I cannot remember Merrill Hinckley, but I have known two of his sons, Max and Gale, and his grandson, Jerry. I can remember Mr. Merrill and his four daughters. I saw the black-gowned Mrs. Merrill Hinckley in church every Sunday. In the days of my girlhood, Mrs. Frank Merrill was one of the ladies I most admired.

When I was four or five years old, I often went with Grandfather Maddocks to the Merrill and Hinckley store.

His fat Brownie drew us there. When we arrived at the store, Grandpa took great pains in hitching the horse. He chose a hitching post away from any other posts because he feared that another horse might kick Brownie. He covered the horse with netting in summer, a blanket in winter. Grandfather always carried produce to the store and sometimes a molasses jug. He had no hand for his little granddaughter. He used to say to me, "You hold on to the end of Grandpa's jacket. Don't leave go of it and don't speak unless you are spoken to." So where Grandfather went, there went I.

Grandpa first delivered his butter and eggs to Mr. Merrill or to young Max, who was very handsome. Then he read off the list of things that Grandma wanted, a few groceries and perhaps a spool of thread. Once a month, Grandfather brought the molasses jug to be filled. Before following Mr. Merrill or Max to the warm cellar where were stored hogsheads of molasses, vinegar, and barrels of flour, Grandfather stopped at the open cracker barrel and took out two crackers, one for himself and one for me. In the cellar the great molasses barrel lay on its side in a wooden frame. There was a spigot in the head of the barrel and from the spigot the storekeeper dribbled molasses on our crackers. If Grandfather liked the flavor and the sweetness of the molasses, he said, "Fill the jug, please." If he was not pleased, he said, "Not quite up to snuff. I'll wait for the next consignment of molasses."

Our last call in the store was at the candy counter. Both Grandpa and I had a sweet tooth. At the counter he bought three rolls of lozenges, one for Grandma, one for himself, and one for me. When we left the store, either Mr. Merrill or Max opened the door for us. If it was Max, he was sure to say something to me. I felt that his words allowed me to break my grandfather's decree of silence. If it was Mr. Merrill who opened the door, the last words were addressed to my grandfather: "Nice little girl you have there. Someday she will have to come to play with my Hilda."

When I was six or seven years old, I went weekly with my father to the store at East Blue Hill. Mother did not go with us. But she made out the grocery list and sped us on our way with directions: "Now, Esther, you stay right near your father. You watch her, John. Buy only the items on the list. Don't buy a lot of candy." Father responded with a gracious inclination of his head and a quick wave of his hand.

The ride to East Blue Hill was mostly downhill. Prince needed no urging to go at a swift pace. Father pointed out the spots of interest: the row of mailboxes at the top of Mailbox Hill, boxes of the workers who worked in the quarries and sheds of the Chase Granite Company; the road to the York Shore; the location of Father's woodlots; the schoolhouse where he had once taught a term of school; the spot at the head of the cove where Grandfather Wood's *Meridian* had been built. When we reached the store, Father hitched Prince to a post and covered him if it was raining or if it was cold. He lifted me out over the wheel of the buggy and I ran ahead of him into the store. Sometimes I alerted Mr. Long and his son to our arrival by calling out, "Papa and I are here."

If there were people in the chairs around the stove, I rushed up to speak to them. In winter, when there were no visitors around the stove, I spit on the hot stovetop. If the store cat was napping on the dry goods counter, I took pains to wake him. I interested myself in the open containers about the store, stirring up the beans in the barrels, the yellow eyes and the red kidneys. I stuck a finger into the pail of peanut butter and drew out a finger-taste of the spread. I treated myself to a cracker from the cracker barrel and a pickle from the pickle crock. With a long-handled fork I speared a string of pickled hot dogs floating in a cask of brine, and then let the string fall back into the brine.

When Father went to the back store with Mr. Long to get kerosene for our lamps and grain for the barn bins, I chose to stay in the main store with young Ross Long. While Ross busied himself with a customer or the store's books, I entertained myself with the thread chest, a container of six drawers that held spools of thread of various degrees of fineness and of various colors. The fineness did not interest me but the colors did. I loved to look at all the shades of pink and purple, blue and green, red and yellow. I ignored the spools of white, black, and brown thread. I not only looked at the spools, I rearranged a few, just to see how a spool of pink thread looked in a yellow row, how a spool of red thread looked in a green row.

Courtesy of J. M. Hinckley

When I tired of the thread chest, I went to the candy assortment displayed in a glass case of several shelves. The Longs prided themselves on their offerings of candy. There was a tray of "baked beans," peanuts covered with a coating of red sugar. There were ice-cream drops — mounds of chocolate-covered white fondant. There were Necco wafers and lozenges, and sugar hearts with polite expressions of affection on them; peanut brittle, needhams, gumdrops, licorice, bonbons, cinnamon pills, orange slices, sugar balls. At Christmastime the Longs sold ribbon candy and candy canes.

When Father came back from the outer store and noticed me in front of the candy case, he was sure to say to Ross, "Fill Esther's candy order, please. I could stand a ten-cent order or even a fifteen-cent order."

Our last chore in the store was the selection of a gift for Mother. Father used to say, "No sense to buy her candy because Daughter and I would eat most of it." We usually bought Mother a few sticks of rick-rack or cloth for aprons or linen for towels.

When we left the store, either Ross or Mr. Long opened the door for us. If it was Ross who opened the door, he winked at me. If it was Mr. Long, he scowled. Neither echoed Mr. Merrill's words, "Nice little girl."

I was eleven or twelve years old before I became acquainted with Mr. Twining's store, which stood beside the village sawmill. My neighbor Emily and I were then students in the village grammar school in the old Academy building. We usually walked home after the day's session. We were expected to wait for Emily's younger brothers, who were in the intermediate school up the hill from the Twining store. Emily and I usually went inside to wait for George and Oscar. Emily shuddered at the cuspidors beside the stove. I took pains to give my name to Nathan Twining, the proprietor, a man of few words and a pale face. He replied to me with a wan smile, remarking, "Oh, yes, you are John Wood's daughter."

I never felt at home with Mr. Twining. I was glad when he was in the office and Mr. Parker was behind the counter. Mr. Parker always knew just what to say to Emily and me and soon he had us laughing. When a customer came in and Mr. Parker was busy, Emily and I walked in front of the shelves and read the names on the cans. The boys soon came running in just as Emily began to worry about them, thinking that they had stopped to play at the Mill Brook or gone to the sawmill to watch the men at work.

In my childhood, the Blue Hill grocery stores were places where men met to gossip, reminisce, and talk politics; where grandfathers and grandchildren, fathers and children were companions; where big children waited for little brothers. They were more than places to buy and sell.

3

Native Teachers

THE FIRST TEACHERS in Blue Hill were men. The first school-rooms were rooms in homes.

Hannah Wood, born in 1844, first went to school in her grandmother's front room. Her first teacher was Allen Wood, a cousin of Grandfather Giles Wood. She used to tell me how the bleating of the sheep and the mooing of the cows diverted the children from their lessons; how the smell of baking gingerbread made them raise their heads from their slates. The schoolmaster had lost a leg in his childhood and wore an artificial leg that fascinated the children. The boys now and then jabbed a pin into it. It was an unfortunate lad who one day jabbed the wrong leg.

Sometime in the early fifties, a schoolhouse was built at Friend's Corner. It was situated at the foot of a hill that at once was called Schoolhouse Hill. The building had a door in the side facing the road, an end chimney, and three windows. The house has long been gone but the large door rock marks its location. Heard Lord was one of the masters who taught there. He drove or walked the two and a half miles from his home to the school. Mr. Lord liked music and when he saw that his pupils were becoming bored or tired, he said, "Children, put aside your books. We'll sing awhile." He took his harmonica from his pocket, sounded a few notes, and started the children on a song. Joel Closson, who lived in the house across the street from the schoolhouse, had a strong, sweet tenor and sometimes the master asked him to sing alone.

Schoolmasters who were Heard Lord's contemporaries were Jedediah Holt, Amos Allen, and Moses Pillsbury. The three gave up teaching and became Baptist preachers. I do not know what they taught, but I do know what Moses Pillsbury studied when he went to school in the village academy. A friend loaned me young Pillsbury's homemade notebook, dated 1816. It has thirty-five pages and is neatly divided into sections: Heights and Distances; Leases, Articles of Agreement; Receipts; Surveying; Projects on the Equator; Geometry; Navigation. The handwriting is excellent. Numerous pen-and-ink drawings add interest to the book. These are sketches of a tower, a church, a house, globes, geometric figures, and ships. In the book is a loose slip of paper that the teacher failed to give to the pupil:

Bluehill March 20th, 1841
This may certify that Augustus W. Clough has excelled his class in spelling the present week.
M. Pillsbury, Instructor

It is possible that my grandfather, Giles Johnson Wood, was a student in Mr. Pillsbury's classroom. I do know that Giles Wood went to Blue Hill Academy and, like many boys of the town who hoped to go to sea, took a course in navigation. I have the book that he used. It is *The Practical Navigator and Seaman's New Daily Assistant* by John Moore, published in London in 1791. The inside of the cover bears the names of earlier owners: Charles Cabot, Hosea Beckwith, and Giles Johnson.

Men were teaching in Blue Hill schools as late as the last decades of the nineteenth century and the start of the twentieth century. But they usually left teaching for some other line of work. R. G. F. Candage became a sea captain; John Wood, a granite cutter; Eugene Stover, a missionary and preacher; Frank Maddocks, a mining engineer.

In the early decades of this century, teaching seemed to run in certain families. There lived on South Street three McIntyre families. The nine daughters of the three families taught school. Four of them were lifetime teachers. Five of the eight children of Judge and Mrs. Edward Chase became teachers.

By the 1890s, most of the teachers received some educa-

Courtesy of Robert Sweetall

tion beyond the academy. A few went to Coburn Classical Institute in Waterville or to the Methodist Seminary in Bucksport. But most went to the Eastern State Normal School in Castine. After a term or two there, a young woman taught a rural school, usually in her home town. My first three teachers in the school at Friend's Corner were under twenty, without teaching experience, and had had only one term at Castine. But they were fine teachers because they had enthusiasm and originality.

By the 1920s, young women were leaving their home towns and going to other towns to teach. Two of the Condon sisters of Brooksville taught in Blue Hill. They were full of fun and music and they played baseball with their pupils. They usually went home weekends, but when they did not go home they were sure of invitations to stay in the homes of admiring students. Some Blue Hill women went to teach in Massachusetts cities. They went when they were young; they summered in Blue Hill; when they were old, they came home to stay.

In every generation there is an outstanding teacher. Nellie Douglass of Blue Hill was such a teacher. She was born in 1881, of Scotch ancestry. She taught in both the grammar school and Blue Hill Academy. As a young woman, she lived at the top of Tenney Hill and cared for an aging grandmother. In later years she cared for an aged mother and lived in the beautiful old house almost opposite the Old Cemetery. From it she could see both the mountain and the bay. She had retired before I went to the village to school, but I used to see her often because she visited school. When I met her on the sidewalk, she stopped me to ask about my lessons. She was tall and slender, with gray hair and red cheeks. When she spoke to me, her sharp eyes gleamed. Sometimes she asked me, "Are you doing as well as you can in school?"

My cousin Austin went to school to Miss Douglass and he told me stories that pointed up her quick wit and sense of humor. One day when she was reading aloud to her students, one of her garters came loose and dropped with a loud plop on the floor of the platform. She finished the sentence she was reading, bent sedately to pick up the garter, and primly said, "There! I am always dropping my bookmark."

When Academy students had a social, Miss Douglass was often the chaperone. One day when Cousin Austin went into Merrill and Hinckley's store, Max Hinckley said to him, "Why don't you see Miss Douglass home from the social tonight? I'll give you fifty cents if you will do so." Fifty cents was no mean amount in 1916. Austin agreed to the storekeeper's proposition. After the evening social, he approached the teacher and asked, "Miss Douglass, may I see you home?" The teacher made a brisk reply, "I accept your offer." Student and pupil found much to talk about on the short walk to the Douglass home. After the teacher had unlocked her door, she turned to Austin and asked, "How did you happen to ask to walk home with me?" When he told her of Max and his proposition, she laughed and said, "That Max! He has never grown up. He is as full of mischief as he was when he was in my seventh grade."

Miss Douglass herself could be full of fun. She and her neighbor, Dr. Littlefield, often played jokes with each other. One morning she saw the doctor seated in his Ford in front of the post office. He was reading the paper. She approached the car quietly, clapped the doctor on the shoulder, and said, "Hello, you toothless fool!" The paper was abruptly lowered. Miss Douglass found that she was face to face with the new superintendent of schools who, like Dr. Littlefield, owned a Model T.

I have known women who were once in Miss Douglass's

classes. One of them used to say to me, "You can tell one of Nellie Douglass's students. She taught us to speak loudly, distinctly, and positively."

Mary Ellen Chase was one of Miss Douglass's students. When Miss Douglass died in 1942, Miss Chase wrote a tribute to her. I quote a portion of it:

> She knew how to inspire her students with respect for good, careful work and hatred for the slipshod and unworthy. She said that a thing worth doing is worth doing well. We respected her so deeply that we literally did not dare to fail in any task which she set before us, just as we did not dare to fail her in our manners, in our respect for older people and in our sense of what is decent and seemly in behavior. She set an example which even young people could feel toward their village, their church, their school and their families. She exacted the best from us because we were always conscious that she herself gave nothing except her best.

Mildred Chase Hinckley was for several decades the outstanding teacher at Stevens Academy. She was a widow who lived with her mother while her son was away at preparatory school and college. She was slender, with graying hair that she kept back from her face by combs. She usually wore a skirt and shirtwaist. Her collar was always fastened with a brooch or bar. I recall that she had a cameo, an opal pin, and a gold bar in the shape of a riding whip.

It is hard to define the qualities that made her a great teacher. She was not a strong disciplinarian. She did not have a fine speaking voice. She was not a storyteller. She was not adept at turning an amusing phrase. She did not try innovations. She did not entertain or amuse us. She was gentle, a bit withdrawn, and she never, never attempted to make herself popular with her pupils.

I believe that her success in teaching came from her presence and her expectations. She was unmistakably a lady. She was plainly a woman who worked hard. She had great expectations for her students.

I was only an average student. But I caught Mrs. Hinckley's enthusiasm for Latin grammar. I spent hours with Allyn and Greenough's book. When I was a freshman at Colby College, the professor asked me to stay after class. When we were alone, he asked, "Who was your Latin teacher?" When I told him, he said, "When you go home, give her my congratulations and tell her that I seldom find a student as well prepared in Latin grammar as you are." His words gave me what every young person needs — the sweet feeling of success.

I know what Mrs. Hinckley did for me. Likely she did different things for different students. But she certainly encouraged in all her students a desire to succeed.

I never taught in a Blue Hill school. I am the poorer for not having done so. But I did attend school for twelve years in Blue Hill. Father, Mother, and Aunt Fannie Maddocks taught in Blue Hill schools. Uncle Frank, A. D. Gray, an uncle by marriage, and four great-aunts taught school. It was no wonder that schools were a favorite topic of conversation at family gatherings. The teacher, the schoolhouse, the parents, the students, and the schoolbooks all came under discussion. Sad tales and glad were told. When the holiday reunion was over, when the long Sunday afternoon closed, and it was time to go home, Father always had the last words: "What makes a good school is a good teacher."

4

Blue Hill Food

BLUE HILL PEOPLE have always been interested in food.

We insist that our favorite foods be cooked the way our forebears cooked them. The addition of tomatoes, peas, and carrots to clam chowder we regard as contamination. We insist that blueberries are for pies, cakes, and muffins; that berries have no place in gelatin desserts and ice cream. Homemade "'east bread" is a Blue Hill favorite. We regard the sprinkling of loaf tops with caraway seeds, nuts, or onion rings as near sacrilege.

Blue Hill people are fish-eaters, but our tastes have changed with the decades. I believe that we eat some fish because of local loyalty, not because of the taste. Pickled herring and smoked alewives (pronounced "L wives") are examples. The former was never served in our home. My friend Emily recalls that there was always a crock of pickled fish in the Clay cellar. On the rare occasions when her mother served the fish, she softened the blow by making hot biscuits and topping the cake with extra-thick frosting.

Every spring my father bought a string of smoked alewives from the store in Surry. They had been caught in Surry; they had been smoked in Surry; they were Surry's best. The string hung in the shed for days and scented the room with the odor of burning alders. At father's urging, Mother finally steamed some of the fish. Father, loyal to the foods of his childhood, declared, "These are every bit as good as those that Zenas Closson used to smoke." I noticed that Mother ate few of the fish and gave no alewive testimonial. When Father forgot all about the alewives, Mother boiled them and fed them to the hens. The alewive odor lingered in the shed long after their bones had disappeared from the henyard.

Blue Hill people once preferred codfish to haddock. Cod fishermen called the haddock "white eyes" and threw them back into the water. In the 1870s, when finnan haddie was introduced, haddock suddenly became popular. Lobster was not popular in the mid-nineteenth century. Hannah Wood said that lobsters were boiled, crushed, and fed to the hens in her childhood. Boys picked up a few of the shellfish at low tide and took them to the Head-of-the-Bay where villagers bought them for two cents each.

Before fresh fish were sold from door to door and sold in the stores, people dried codfish. Pieces of the "stripped fish" were torn off, soaked in water, and then boiled. People called it "Cape Cod turkey" and ate it with white sauce, pork scraps, and baked potatoes. Later they bought salted cod put up in wooden boxes. They boiled it to make fish hash and chowder. Clams, used in stews and chowders or fried, have always been popular in Blue Hill. But the fritters, so popular in the 1890s, are neglected today. Clams were once plentiful on the flats. It was said of very poor families, "They wintered out by living off the clam flats."

Men and women of my father's generation did not eat tuna. Father spoke for his contemporaries when he declared, "Never, never will I eat horse mackerel." Mother had little use for cusk. In later years when the stores sold fish and Father was going to the store, Mother used to say to him, "Don't get cusk. It is not worth buying. It is not worth bringing home. It is not worth cooking." Today we eat both tuna and cusk and call them good.

Two prejudices of earlier days linger. Fried eels are not popular. One of my friends used to say, "I don't like eels. They wiggle in the frying pan." I like eels, but for years I would not eat mussels. My neighbor ordered me to eat them and to like them. One day at suppertime she brought in a little stewpan filled with hot mussel stew. She said to me, "Now don't be prejudiced. Eat them and you'll like them." I ate them. I liked them. Ever since I have smacked my lips over mussels.

Blue Hill people have decided views about baked beans. We hold that beans should be given a slow baking, preferably in an old beanpot in a wood-burning stove. Salt, mustard, brown sugar, lean salt pork, and a dollop of molasses should be the companions of the beans. Ketchup, hot dogs, and onions have no place in a Blue Hill beanpot. We are particular about dry beans used for baking. Jacob's cattle, red kidney, soldier, and yellow eyes are our favorites. Pea beans are a second choice. No Blue Hiller would choose to eat baked lima beans. The bread served with baked beans should be homemade yeast bread, brown bread, or johnnybread. Biscuits or muffins are acceptable. Sweet coffee cake and tea breads are totally unacceptable.

Blue Hillers like hash, three kinds of hash: fish, meat, and red flannel. There is a threefold secret to making good hash. The ingredients should be chopped and not put through a grinder. And they should be chopped very, very fine. The hash should be cooked in an old iron frying pan with pork scraps. It is best cooked on an iron stove where the frying pan is first placed on a very hot front cover and then moved to a back cover. Once the lower crust is brown, half the hash should be flipped over the other half. Cooks do not always agree on the details of hash making. Some choose to mold the hash into balls or cakes. Most choose cod for fish hash. But my mother always said that the best fish hash is made of halibut with cream used in the mixture. Some serve dropped eggs on red flannel hash that is made of the leftovers from a boiled dinner. Many cooks served fish hash or fish cakes for Sunday dinner. The hash or cakes were prepared on Saturday and fried once the family got home from church and Sunday school.

We natives like pies. But in the days of weight watchers, fewer pies are baked. No one liked pies better than my Grandfather Maddocks. Every October he asked Grandma, "Ellie, how is our supply of pie stock?" She knew what he meant and always gave him an optimistic answer: "Even better than usual. The squash, pumpkins, and cranberries will last until January. The apples will last until mid-April. The mincemeat crock is full. If the hens lay eggs and the cow gives milk, I'll be able to make custard and chocolate and sour cream pies." The last was one of Grandpa's favorites. It is a custardlike pie with chopped raisins in it.

Blue Hill people eat fewer cakes than they once did. One of Mother's cookbooks, published in 1911, has eleven pages devoted to cake recipes. A 1988 cookbook published in western Maine has only six pages of cake recipes. The names of the cakes that I find in old cookbooks suggest that many of the cakes were very rich and very sweet. Here are a few of the mouth-watering names: Hundred-Dollar Chocolate Cake, Chocolate-Nougat Cake, World's Fair Cake, Walnut-Cream Cake, and Chocolate Coconut Cake. Layer cakes, once the pride of church suppers, are now extinct. I was sad to be told that there are children who have never eaten whipped cream cake.

A Blue Hill gardener has his vegetable favorites. He prefers Hubbard squashes to the recently produced varieties. He prefers chard to kale and endive. He likes cabbage but has no use for brussels sprouts. He has little enthusiasm for broccoli, none for eggplant. Peas, corn, beans, carrots, beets, and potatoes are the standbys in a Maine garden. Tomatoes are raised for summer eating and fall pickling. But the gardener prefers to raise tomatoes that are large and red. He chooses to ignore the varieties that are unusual in shape or color or size.

A Blue Hill native knows that in order for the food to be good, the ingredients have to be good. A cook's attention is always focused on five ingredients: molasses (does it have the proper flavor?); salt pork (is it fresh and lean?); milk (is it fresh and flavorful?); apples (are they crisp and tasty?); potatoes (are they firm and mealy?)

Blue Hill people show their interest in food by talking about it. Second only to weather, food is our favorite topic of conversation.

5

Blue Hill Cooks

GRANDMA MADDOCKS USED TO SAY, "I cook just as my mother used to cook. My pantry is like her pantry. Her table and her rocker are in my kitchen."

Grandma's pantry was a narrow room at the end of the ell. Its one window, above the sink, looked out on the head of the cove and the curve in the Sand Hill. To the left of the sink were open shelves on which were pots and pans, spiders and bowls. To the right of the sink was an area used for preparation. The part beside the sink was kept free of dishes except when Grandma was cooking. Under it was a cupboard in which were four firkins. One held sugar; another, salt; the third, cornmeal; and the fourth, crackers. The remainder of the shelf held the flour board, always ready for service with the flour sieve, cooking bowl, and big spoon. Above the flour board was the cupboard that held the seasonings, the flavorings, the tea and coffee. Under the flour board was a doorless space in which was stored a barrel holding one hundred ninety-six pounds of flour. It could be swung out so Grandma could reach into it.

At the end of the pantry, the coffee grinder was on the wall. Under it stood a jug of molasses and a jug of vinegar. The grinder was used every morning to grind the beans for the breakfast coffee. There was a cupboard beside the door to the kitchen where were stored Grandma's everyday dishes, white ironstoneware. Under the sink were kept the dishpan, a container of soft soap, which was made by Grandmother, and a wooden container with two compartments. The center board that divided the compartments curved high to make a handle. This knife and fork container was dear to Grandmother. When she was getting ready to cook, she used to say to me, "Get out the old holder. You know that your great-grandfather Grindle bought it for your great-grandmother the year they were married. In those days a dry cooper from Bucksport drove from door to door selling his holders and firkin."

Grandma's kitchen was more sitting room than cooking room. In it were her sewing machine, a calico-covered nail keg holding papers and magazines, a plant stand, Great-grandmother's kitchen table, the cat's chair, two straight chairs, and two rockers. Beside one of the outside doors was the woodbox with padded cover, which, lowered, changed the box into a settee. On the floor were hooked and braided rugs demoted from bedroom use.

The baking was done in the kitchen where a great "six-holer" iron stove dominated the room. On its top were two kettles, one of black iron and the other of bright copper. Behind the stove was a long shelf on which were a hen's wing, used to brush the hearth, three hand lamps, and a wooden "stick" designed to stir hasty pudding. When I was a small child, the match holder stood high on a pantry shelf.

The landing at the head of the cellar stairs was an adjunct to the kitchen and pantry. On its floor were three pottery jars: one held bread; one, doughnuts; one, cookies. Beside the jars were the filled molasses jug and a cake firkin. On the wall of the cellarway there were shelves on which Grandma stored cooked meat and leftover vegetables and pies. She never had an icebox. In summer she stored food in the cool cellar.

Grandmother Maddocks used to say, "My cellar is not as big as my mother's was but it holds as many good things as did hers." Grandfather every fall saw to it that cellar boxes and barrels were filled with vegetables and apples. There were boxes of potatoes, carrots, beets, and turnips. There were barrels of "Macs" for early winter use.There were barrels of Moose Rivers for baking and barrels of Bellflowers, Baldwins, Nodheads, and Peewalkees for late-winter pies and sauce. Near the base of the chimney was the pork barrel, filled with brine in which floated pieces of salt pork. Beside it was an old footstool, placed there for my use. I loved to stand on the stool and with a long-handled fork spear a piece of pork to cook with Saturday night's beans.

Not far from the pork barrel were hanging shelves on which were preserves and jelly. Grandma belonged to a generation that did not can vegetables and make marmalade. She stored the preserves and jelly in an orderly fashion. The strawberries, the cherries, the blueberries, the plums, the raspberries, and the blackberries, each had its own enclave. The currant jelly and gooseberry jelly did not touch shoulders. Nor did the elderberry and the apple, the mint and the quince. Grandmother assigned special shelves to her pickles: the dill and the ripe cucumber; the mustard and piccalilli; the sweet and the sour; the beet and the corn relish.

The kitchen had two doors. One faced the bay and the steep slope to the road. This door was seldom used or unlocked. Between it and the kitchen was a small hall that Grandmother used as a closet. Here was stored the churn that saw service every Thursday. Here was kept the rag bag and the rug-frame that usually held a half-completed rug. Here were stored sweaters, raincoats, rubbers, and over-shoes. The back door of the kitchen was beside the woodbox and it saw constant service because it was near the barn, the woodshed, the driveway, the henhouses, and the orchard. Outside the door was a "built-on" structure that Grandma aimed to keep in perfect order.

The cellar was not the only storeroom that Grandmother had for winter food. The room over the ell had never been finished and was used as a keeping room. In it were stacks of Grandfather's *Rural New Yorkers* and *New England Home-steads* and Grandmother's *Modern Priscillas*. Hanging from the rafters were strings of dried apples and pumpkins and bunches of sage. On the floor under the end of the window were pumpkins, some of which were used for cow feed, and squash. Nearby were lard pails filled with cranberries that Grandfather had picked on the wet margins of the brook.

On Candlemas Day, Grandfather always said to Grand-mother, "Half your meat and half your hay." That was a reminder for Grandmother to check her supplies. By that time the cranberries, the squash, the pumpkins, and the "Macs" were gone. But other things were usually holding out well. At dinnertime Grandmother reported, "Well, Levi, I've checked around. We have enough to last us over to garden sass, berries, and early apples."

Grandmother, unlike many of her contemporaries, did not dry herbs for winter use. She dried no pennyroyal for stomachaches; no mullein for cough syrup; no lavender for sachet bags. But she did take care to try out "hen's oil" from hen's fat. She combined the "oil" with camphorated oil and poured the mixture into bottles. When a member of her family had a chest cold, he slept with his chest covered with a flannel cloth covered with the ointment.

When Grandmother said, "I cook just as my mother did," she likely meant that she used her mother's recipes that she knew from memory. Once a week she made yeast bread, always using white flour. My mother recalled that in her childhood her mother used potato yeast. When Mother went to the Academy, it was her Friday task to buy a cup of the fluid yeast for five cents from Mrs. Gross, the wife of the village barber. When Mother complained about the bother of taking a cup to school and the inconvenience of bringing home the mixture, Grandmother put her in her place and said, "Now don't you fuss. Selling the homemade yeast is Mrs. Gross's one way of earning spending money and I am glad to help her out." By the time of my childhood, Grandmother had come to use store-purchased yeast cakes. But she never consented to use graham or whole-wheat flour that her daughters recommended to her.

Grandmother used yeast for bread but not for doughnuts. Her doughnut "rule" called for the use of a cup of hot mashed potato. Her doughnuts were yellow with egg yolks and light as a feather. I liked to stand at her elbow when she fried them so that I could eat the first one taken from the bubbling fat. It was hot and crisp and so delicious that I always asked for a second.

Grandmother made great use of corn and cornmeal and she hulled corn, using the corn from the grain room in the barn. Hulling was a long and hard process, but Grandpa liked hulled corn and Grandma cooked to please him. She used cornmeal to make johnnycake, drowned corn bread, and brown bread. She used the meal to make hasty pudding, a Sunday-night dish that required a long afternoon of cooking and was best when covered with cream.

Molasses was one of Grandfather's favorite foods. He liked it on hot biscuits and pancakes. He liked a big dollop of it cooked with baked beans. He liked it in gingerbread, not one kind of gingerbread, but two: soft and hard. Often there were two plates of gingerbread on the supper table. I always hoped that the soft kind would be near my place. I did not like the hard gingerbread, also called "muster gingerbread." It contained more ginger, less sweetening, and less shortening than the soft kind. But Grandfather always smacked his lips over it and declared, "Just like that my grandmother used to make for Uncle Moses and Father when they went to Bucksport to drill in the militia."

When Grandmother mixed a cake, she sat in her mother's rocking chair. She held the great yellow mixing bowl in her lap and she beat and beat. She was never in a hurry. She loved to cook and she liked to make the task last as long as possible. As she beat the batter, she rocked; she talked to Duffy, asleep in his chair; she looked out the window at the bay; she admired her houseplants. And she repeated poetry, matching her beating to the rhythm of the verse.

Grandmother was not without originality in her cooking. She was firm in observing her rule, never cook wild strawberries. When she made wild strawberry pie, she crushed the berries, poured the red mixture into a pie shell, and topped the pie with whipped cream. For some reason, she baked squash pie in a square cake pan. I was always careful to remark, "I hope that I don't get the center piece because I like lots of crust with pie." She made a supper dish that no one else made. She poured a mixture of bread crumbs, cheese, and egg yolks, beaten, into custard cups, topped the cups with beaten egg whites, and baked the mixture in a quick oven. When her family tired of eating fried smelts, she cooked the little fish in a beanpot filled with brine made of water, vinegar, and spices. The bones dissolved in a long oven-baking and the flavor of the dish was delicious.

Grandmother's friends and family liked her cooking, whether she cooked from memory or from imagination. When they complimented her, she always answered, "Thank you, but all I do is to cook just as my mother did."

When Great -aunt Fan heard Grandma declare her devotion to the culinary practice of her mother, Aunt Fan remarked, "Well, I do not cook just as my mother did. Not at all! I intend to keep up to date in my housekeeping and cooking."

Aunt Fan subscribed to the *Delineator*, the *Woman's Home Companion,* and *The Ladies Home Journal*. These magazines increased her desire for change. She discarded the iron sink in the kitchen and had a slate one put in. She had her kitchen shelf covered with zinc. She was one of the first natives to buy an icebox. The new purchase was set in the shed. Its drainpipe was connected to a larger drainpipe so that Aunt never had to empty the drip pan. She did have a long trip to the icebox from the kitchen through the back hall, across the end of the porch to the shed. Aunt Fan was the first of the great-aunts to substitute place mats for tablecloths and bread-and-butter plates for butter chips. She was the first to use tinned oysters and canned pineapple.

Aunt Fan prided herself on serving "something different" at the holiday dinner table. My Grandfather Maddocks was critical of what he called "Fan's newfangled ideas." He did not hesitate to express his disappointment when pecan pie took the place of pumpkin pie and canned asparagus was substituted for boiled onions. He refused to eat either stuffed celery or grated carrots.

Grandfather took a more tolerant view of his sister's layer cakes, made from *Delineator* recipes and served on a pedestal cut-glass dish. He liked her "Hundred-Dollar Chocolate Cake" and her "Caramel Coconut Mountain Cake." He voiced his approval by the declaration, "Good enough to make hair grow on a bald head."

Some of Aunt Fan's new ideas came from the Mutual Benefit column of the *Ellsworth American*. The column was edited by Mary Mayo, the wife of Eben Mayo, one of the town's master carpenters. Mrs. Mayo encouraged her readers to send in recipes and letters for her to use in her column. Aunt Fan and three of her sisters, Maria Ginn, Mary Burrill, and Louise Leach, were frequent contributors. Some years Mrs. Mayo sponsored a picnic for those who had sent in stories or recipes.

Mary Mayo was more than a pioneer columnist and a good cook. She played the organ in the Blue Hill Congregational Church and wrote both music and songs as well as verse. She was always ready to write and recite a poem for a wedding, an anniversary, or an historical observance.

My mother was a good cook. She used to say, "I cook just as my mother did." But I recall that she borrowed Aunt Fan's women's magazines and read the M. B. column in the *Ellsworth American*.

6

The Storytellers

IN MY CHILDHOOD I loved to listen to a story — a long story or a short one, a sad or a happy one, an exciting story or a quiet one, a story about folks at home or strangers at sea. They were all welcome to me.

One of the storytellers of my childhood told me about people whom she had known in her childhood of the 1880s. Her stories never had an ending. They left questions unanswered. She liked to tell me about a carpenter who never worked for an employer more than a few weeks. She used to say, "He worked hard and he worked with skill, but all the time he sang very loudly, off pitch and out of tune. The other workmen threatened to quit unless the singer were fired." Fired he was and he stayed at home to hoe the garden and tend the cows. His singing startled the birds in the garden and frightened the cattle in the pasture. When he walked to the village on an errand, his singing alerted people to his passing. When I asked the storyteller, "Why was he always singing?" she answered, "That I never knew."

A second story she told me concerned a neighbor of the singing carpenter. She called him "Mr. X," but I suspected whom she meant. The man lived when the sale of liquor in Maine was prohibited by law. "Mr. X" liked liquor and he knew where to purchase it on the sly. Once a week he hitched his driving horse up and drove down to the village. If he met a person in a carriage or afoot, if he saw a person at work in a nearby yard, he pulled up the horse and made a formal announcement: "I'm on my way to the Baptist dining room. My wife left her pie plate there after the last church supper. I'm on my way to get the plate." This story made no sense to me but I knew that it was no use to ask the storyteller for an explanation.

She told another story that was even more puzzling. Near "Mr. X" there lived a man who had the burden of an alcoholic wife. He bore his burden bravely. On the evenings when his wife was drunk and asleep on the sofa, he covered her with a quilt. Then he hitched up the best horse and drove to the village church where he tied the horse in the churchyard. He walked to the home of a woman of whom he was enamored. Covered with sheets, man and woman walked in the cemetery. I felt that this story had undertones of which Mama would not approve. I asked for no explanations.

My father was a master hand at retelling a story. My mother used to say to him, "John, you never tell a story twice the same way. You are always adding facts or changing details." He had a quick answer: "Lizzie, that is what they call literary license." When my cousins and I were very young, we were always asking Father to tell the story of Grandfather Wood's pig. It was a tale that he told with infinite variety. He recalled that one year in the 1870s, when Captain Wood hauled up his schooner for the winter, he had a quarrel with the first mate, Jairus Osgood. It was customary for the mate to cut canvas from a bolt owned by the captain. The mate was expected to use the cloth to make palms to protect his hands and ditty bags to hold his odds and ends. This voyage Jairus had used no canvas. So the last day aboard, he cut off several yards of canvas to take home to his wife, Elizabeth. He said that it was his due, but the captain insisted that the canvas was meant to be used for articles used aboard ship, not ashore. Jairus won out and went home with canvas as a gift for his wife.

Captain Wood went home but he did not forget about the argument with his mate. Whenever he went to the village, he called at the Osgood home. Early in March, he came home with a very small pig from the Osgood barn. The captain and his two little boys enjoyed taking care of the pig and often talked about the pig's growth and strong lungs. Mrs. Wood noticed that the captain and the older boy smiled and winked at each other whenever the pig was mentioned. One day, she drew her younger son aside and said to him, "Now, Johnnie, you tell me all about your father's pig." Johnnie was glad to oblige. As a starter he announced, "Piggie has a queer name. It's Canvas-back."

Eliza Wood let no grass grow under her feet. She hunted up her husband and demanded, "Did you pay Jairus for the pig?" The captain's quick answer was, "No, and I don't intend to pay him. I am taking the pig to make up for his taking the canvas."

Eliza knew how to manage her husband. She broke into loud weeping. Between her sobs she mourned, "You are teaching your little boys to be dishonest."

Right away the captain drove to town and paid for the pig. When he got back home, he remarked to his younger son, "John, you gave me away. Now I'll always be out of pocket for three or four yards of canvas."

Uncle Arthur liked to tell funny stories and he laughed at them. He liked best to tell stories in winter before a blazing fire in the sitting room stove, and with his pipe and can of tobacco on the table beside him. He told us how he once swam way out to Long Island, how he had been lost in the woods in a bad snowstorm and had stayed all night in a deserted camp, how he had gone to Concord, New Hampshire, to visit his aunt and returned with a bride.

But we children liked best his story about how a house was built for him. He always started the story the same way: "I don't believe there is another man in town who had a house built for him before he was born." He reminded us that Captain Wood as a young man went to sea eight months of the year and left his young wife, Eliza, to live with her father, John Friend. In the Friend farmhouse she bore two daughters, Hannah in 1844 and Florence in 1846. When Florence died in 1848, the captain decided to take Eliza on a voyage to help her recover from her grief. They went on a small schooner that took lumber to Charleston, South Carolina, and brought back cotton to Brunswick. Eliza discovered that she loved going to sea. She was never seasick. She was never bored. She drew in her sketchbook, read books, and wrote letters. She like to see new places and meet new people. But when she teased little Hannah to go to sea with her, the child answered, "I have to stay with Grandpa and Grandma. They can't spare me."

Eliza went to sea year after year. She saw Rockland, Brunswick, Portland, Portsmouth, Boston, New York,

Charleston, and ports in the Caribbean. But in 1859 her seafaring days came to an end.

When Eliza discovered that she was going to have a baby, she declared, "I'm going to stay at home and take care of this child myself."

The captain made a declaration of his own: "And I am going to build a house for this child."

Uncle Arthur used to tell how John Friend gave land for the house; how a neighbor, Milford Grindle, quarried granite for the underpinning and steps; how timber, cut on the Friend lots, was sawed at the Long mill to make corner posts, sills, beams, flooring, clapboards, and shingles. Bricks for the chimneys and hearths were Blue Hill–made.

Uncle Arthur always ended his story with the reminder, "And don't forget that I was born in the bedroom right off the front hall." If Father was listening to the story, he added, "And don't forget that I was born there six years later."

Arthur Wood and John Wood were good storytellers but their sister Hannah was better. She had grown up at Friend's Corner. As a young girl, she had gone to Concord, New Hampshire, to work in a coat shop. She married Octave Howard and lived with him in Bucksport; Blue Hill; Brattleboro, Vermont; and Rockland. She told stories that her grandfather, born in 1800, had told her. She told about the adventures of her childhood and the trials of family illnesses and deaths. She retold the C. A. Stephens stories that she had read in the *Youth's Companion*. Sometimes she made up her own stories, using the characters of C. A. Stephens.

In my childhood Aunt Hannah visited every summer at Friend's Corner. Sometimes she stayed at the home of Arthur Wood; sometimes, at the home of John Wood. Wherever she stayed, she told stories. Mornings she stayed in the kitchen to help with the cooking and the mending.

Afternoons she sat on our porch or under Uncle's horse chestnut trees and told stories to my cousins and me. Evenings she sat inside the house and told stories for the grown-ups. But we children were there to listen.

Aunt Hannah liked best to talk about her childhood years on her Grandfather Friend's farm. She told how her grandfather took in indentured boys whom her grandmother mothered. She described how her grandfather and her Uncle Otis caught porgies in weirs, boiled them in great iron kettles set over roaring fires, and sold the oil to make paint. She told how her grandmother taught her how to make pillows and pick feathers for pillows from a live goose, to make cheese, and spin yarn. She talked about the school kept in the Friend parlor and the masters who boarded at the Friends'.

Aunt Hannah was always eager to talk about her Uncle Otis. He was musical and beat a drum in the local rallies held for Lincoln in 1860. He fought and died in the Civil War.

But Aunt Hannah was always loath to talk about her mother's other brother, John Friend, Jr., who went to sea. There was an interesting story about this uncle, but Hannah and her brothers did not agree on the ending.

The younger John Friend lived, when he was at home, with his wife, Rebecca, in Blue Hill Village. Now and then they came to Friend's Corner for a meal. John was a silent man and he ignored Hannah. Rebecca was a proud woman and she felt that she had married beneath her. She made it clear that she never intended to go to sea with her husband.

Young John Friend did well as a sailor and finally became first mate on a clipper that sailed out of Portsmouth. A year went by and no word came from the young mate. Then came a short note from the captain of the clipper. He wrote that John Friend had died in China. His father and mother mourned. Rebecca wore black.

Several years later a man from Sedgwick who had been to California came home with a strange story: "On a street in San Francisco, I met John Friend. He hurried by me when I spoke to him and he said, 'I do not know you.'"

Aunt Hannah was always indignant about the story told by the man from Sedgwick. She used to hotly remark, "He lied. Of course the clipper's captain told the truth. Uncle John died in China."

Her brothers had a different ending to the story, "The captain lied to cover up for his first mate. Uncle John jumped ship to be rid of Rebecca. He likely lived a long life in California."

We children were sorry to have Aunt Hannah go home. We missed her daytime stories. One day when Cousin Alice, Cousin Olive, and I were sitting in the shade of the horse chestnut trees, Olive said to me, "Try telling us one of Aunt Hannah's stories. I'll bet you can remember one." I did try and I did remember. I discovered the joy of story-telling and I retold the stories of my father, uncle, and aunt.

Telling stories runs in the Wood family.

7

The Verse-Sayers

My GREAT-AUNT, Fan Parker, enjoyed making up words. Some of them never caught on with the members of the family. Two did: aye-sayer (one who usually agrees with everyone) and verse-sayer (a repeater of verse). Aunt Fan herself was not a verse-sayer. But she did have a rich supply of expressions that I heard no other person use. When everything was going well, she exclaimed, "The goose hangs high." She described a proud person as "a high cock-a-lo-rum." A person whom she distrusted she called "a Doctor Fell." Now and again she made this nonsensical remark: "He's a good man but he can't eat hay."

My Grandmother Maddocks was a verse-sayer. The poems that she repeated were taken from her readers and spelling books and those of her children. She repeated verse for her own enjoyment but only under certain circumstances — when she turned the churn or beat batter, when she brushed and combed her hair, or when she brushed and braided mine. The poems that she recited were either warlike or funereal, although she was a gentle woman who always deferred to the judgment of Grandfather and his five positive-speaking sisters. She remained gentle when she said the lines about "the Assyrians coming down like a wolf on the fold and their cohorts were gleaming with purple and gold." She was gentle when she related the grisly events of "daft McGregor's raids in Costa Rica's everglades." She remained cheerful when she told of the burial of Moses "on Nebo's lonely mountain on this side of Jordan's wave." The details of the burial of Sir John Moore in no way decreased her cheerfulness.

Father, like Grandmother Maddocks, repeated verse for his own pleasure. He could repeat pages of Scott, Longfellow, and Tennyson, but his favorite poet was Burns. His volume of Burns's poems is shabby and worn. When he worked at his bench, he took it with him, and when he weeded the garden, he took it there.

But Father repeated verse for the enjoyment of others. At Grange meetings, Lodge sessions and socials he was always glad to recite one of the Maine dialect poems of Holman Day. He might tell the story of Elkina B. Atkinson, "whose tavurn was run on a plan that was strictly his own," or he might recite the ballad of Ozy B. Orr, "who buckled down to pay up the int'rest and keep off the town." He might repeat the yarn concerning "ole" Lish Henderson, "grouty and gruff, profane and rough," who chose to "play ox."

My Aunt Hannah was the best of all the family verse-sayers. She repeated poems taught to her in her childhood of the 1850s. She repeated the verses she learned from her own schoolbooks and those of her sons, and that she cut out of magazines and papers. She had long years of verse-saying. She repeated poetry to her brothers, who were sixteen and twenty-two years younger than she. She repeated it to her four sons, her eleven grandchildren, and her four great-grandchildren.

She required that her children and grandchildren memorize some of her rhymes. To the end of their days they could say the lines about the parts of speech. These lines end with the announcement,

> Three little words we often see,
> called articles A, An, and The.
> The whole comprise nine parts of speech
> Which reading, writing, speaking teach.

My aunt enjoyed repeating long ballads that had a moral ending. She repeated to very young children the ballad about "the white old hen with yellow legs, who laid her master many eggs." One evening a fox came to the hen-house and tried to get the hen to jump down from the high roost. The hen stayed put. The fox slunk off. The moral of the tale was — do not be fooled by flattery.

To older children Aunt repeated the ballad about the priest and the mulberry tree. The priest was going to a fair on horseback, when he saw a mulberry tree bending with fruit. He turned his horse to the bush, stopped, and stood up in the saddle in order to reach the highest branches of the tree. As "he stood erect on the back of his steed," he said aloud how fortunate he was to have a horse who at a word would stand and at another word would start off. "At the sound of a 'ha,' the horse made a push and away went the priest in the wild briar bush." The punch line of the ballad is: "Much that well may be thought, cannot be wisely said."

My favorite ballad is one about a Quaker, and it begins:

> Early one day in leafy June
> When brooks and birds were all in tune,
> A Quaker on a palfrey brown
> Was riding over Horsely Down.

The Quaker felt safe and secure and was well pleased with himself. He had concealed his money, a considerable amount, in the double sole of his shoe. Unwisely he disclosed the location of his money to a second Quaker whom he met. The second Quaker turned out to be "Captain Bibb, 'the robber trim,'" who was disguised. Bibb took the trusting Quaker's money with these words:

> And for your money I will give advice.
> T'will serve you all your life.
> Don't take each broad brim chance may send
> Though plain his collar for a friend.
> Don't trust in gentleman or clown
> While riding over Horsely Down.

Aunt Hannah had a way of quoting verse to support her point of view. She was very sure that heredity counts for more than environment. Her great-grandchildren may not accept her views, but they certainly remember her often-quoted lines,

> It is not all in bringing up,
> Let folks say what they will.
> Neglect may dim a silver cup.
> It will be silver still.

It is not all in the bringing up,
Let folks say what they will.
Silver wash a pewter cup,
It will be pewter still.

Aunt Hannah's favorite poet was Whittier. Her listeners knew well the stories of Maud Miller, Barbara Frietchie, Cobbler Keezar, and Skipper Ireson.

Children of my generation were verse-sayers. A few of our verses date back to England and Revolutionary Massachusetts:

The Fifth of November, the Fifth of November,
The Gunpowder Treason and Plot.
There is no earthly reason
Why gunpowder and treason
Should ever by us be forgot.

Fee—fi—fo—fum
I smell the blood of an Englishmun
Be he alive or be he dead,
I'll pound his bones to make me bread.

Father taught me two rhymes of his childhood:

But of all poor grub beneath the skies,
The poorest is dried apple pies.
Give me the toothache or sore eyes
In preference to dried apple pies.

Mr. Finney had a turnip
And it grew behind the barn,
And it grew and it grew
And it did no harm.

Mother taught me the lines:

> Monday's child is fair of face.
> Tuesday's child is full of grace.
>   . . .
> But the child that is born on the Sabbath day
> Is loving and giving and blithe and gay.

One of Mother's cousins repeated for my amusement a "days of the week poem" about cutting one's nails:

> Cut your nails on Monday, cut them for wealth.
> Cut them on Tuesday, cut them for health.
>   . . .
> Cut them on Sunday, cut them for evil.
> The whole of the week you'll be ruled by the Devil.

With a perfectly straight face, this cousin used to say to me, "When I was a child, my father never allowed me to cut my nails on Sunday."

We children had various "count out" lines for our games. One of them was vulgar; one was racist. We knew that this one would undergo parental scrutiny:

> Engine, engine Number Nine
> Going down Chicago Line.

We felt more at home when we changed the second line and said, "Coming down the Ellsworth Line."

Everyone, young and old alike, in my childhood, repeated short poems, most of them folk verses. Many of them dealt with the weather:

Night hawks fly low tonight.
Clouds will hide tomorrow's light.

When the stars begin to huddle,
Soon the world will be a puddle.

See a sea glin,
Catch a wet skin.

Some of the verses had a nugget of wisdom:

See a pin and let it lie.
Come to sorrow by and by.

If a task is once begun,
Never leave it 'til it's done.
Be the labor great or small,
Do it well or not at all.

Many were nonsense lines:

This one is about a four-leaf clover:
One is for friendship
And one is for wealth.
One, for a faithful lover
And one to bring you health.
All in a four-leaf clover.

Saturday night dreams, Sunday morning told,
Will come to pass before they're old.

My generation of schoolchildren introduced a nonsense verse into the neighborhood. We were careful not to repeat it in the hearing of our mothers.

> A river of whiskey.
> If I were a duck,
> I'd dive to the bottom
> And I'd never come up.

The verse-sayers handed down the wise lore and nonsense of the past.

Bluehill, Me.

Courtesy of Robert Sweetall

8

The Talkers

MOST OF THE FIRST SETTLERS of Blue Hill came from Andover and Beverly, Massachusetts. They were grandchildren and great-grandchildren of English Puritans who came to the Bay Colony in the seventeenth century. The Puritans had lived in southeastern England and were sailors and village craftsmen, carpenters and printers, furniture makers and weavers. They were brewers, innkeepers, millers, shipbuilders, teachers, and ministers. They spoke with the accent of south coastal England. They brought with them to the Bay colony the vocabulary and the accent of their forebears.

In my childhood we used sea terms, some of which had undergone a land change: back and fill, close quarters, batten down, first rate, aback, aground, afoul, mainstay, headway, above board, and gurry. Even we children knew the difference between the nautical meaning and the ashore meaning of a term.

In my home the vocabulary of cooking had a nautical flavor. Father liked to use the term "grub," a sailor's word for food. Mother frowned upon the use of the word. But she did cook for Father food that was part of a sailor's grub. She made lobscouse, a mixture of meat, onions and hard bread, fried with pork scraps. She made plum duff, one of our favorite desserts. Father always gave the same comment about the duff made by Mother: "This does not seem just like the duff that my father used to make." It was not the same. Captain Wood's duff was a thick flour pudding filled with fruit that he boiled in a cloth bag. Mother steamed squares of hard bread that she combined with dates and figs and apple slices and served with a hot egg sauce.

In our home we called the closet off the dining room the glory hole. It was filled with clothing, boxes, and piles of magazines. In the old days, the glory hole of a ship was an area where gold and valuables were kept. Aboard ship, dunnage meant material strewn under the ballast to protect the ship's planking. Ashore, dunnage meant extra belongings. When Grandma came to spend the day, she brought bags of sewing and gifts. Mother always exclaimed, "Goodness, Mother! You are surely well-laden with dunnage."

Neighborhood slang had a salty taste. We called a naughty child "an Arab," pronounced "Ay-rab." Likely the word went back to the war with the Barbary pirates. We called a slow-moving person "a regular old stick-in-the-mud." Hannah Cook was a term of belittlement. We said of a person, "She is not worth a Hannah Cook." On a sailing craft a hooraw's nest is a tangle of ropes on the deck. Ashore it is a cluttered closet or room. We used the Spanish word "vamoose" to drive the chickens out of the flower garden and the crows out of the corn. We called flattery "palaver," a word taken from the Portuguese "palava." Mother called her button box "my ditty box." She used the term that a sailor applied to the box that held his mending tools.

Sea language enriched the speech of old Blue Hillers. We still speak it, sometimes unaware.

Every generation adds new words to its vocabulary. Every generation drops some of the words used by its forebears.

In my childhood a footstool was called a cricket; an old maid, a spinster; a frying pan, a spider; the cemetery, the yard; the Civil War, the Rebellion; Memorial Day, Decoration Day. We had a rich vocabulary to describe wind and weather: Old Adam's pot is boiling; mackerel sky; a hawk's mouth; a sea glin; the wind backs in; a weather breeder; a fog mull; a pea souper; the line gale; to herm up; pride of the morning; breezen; a catspaw; and a rip-snorter.

People of the early twentieth century sometimes mispronounced words. Thanks to better education and travel, these errors of pronunciation are seldom heard today: "chimbly" for chimney, "fambly" for family, "liberry" for library, "roosberry" for raspberry, "piney" for peony, and "liloc" for lilac. Two mispronunciations have been used so long and so frequently that they are now accepted as correct speech in coastal Maine: "loom" for loam and "ware" for weir.

We Blue Hillers have our own special way of pronouncing place names. We insist that the town of Mariaville is pronounced with only three syllables. The second *a* is silent and the accent is on *ri*. We pronounce Bangor with a heavy accent on the first syllable. We frown on the folks from Aroostook who say "Ban-gér." We like the way we say Bar Harbor. It is regrettable that we coastal people do not agree on the proper way of saying the names Mount Desert and Isle au Haut.

We have a special way of sounding the vowel *a*. We favor a soft rather than a hard *a*. We often ignore an *r*, as we do when we say "deah" for dear. We now and again fail to sound the final *g* of an "ing." I note that sometimes I say to a friend, "I've been cookin' this mornin'," or "I'm goin' to the library this afternoon." Alas! I have been known to place a *g* where none belongs. But I intend to avoid saying "mounting" for mountain.

Blue Hillers of the last years of the nineteenth century were good Victorians. They felt that it was improper to use vulgar or profane language in front of women and children. They worked out a system of profanity substitutes that was still in use into this century. These gave offense to no one: a Jim dandy, I don't give a hoot, plague-gone, by gum, by the great horn spoon, by gorry, by Joe-be, by Godfrey mighty, tarnation, and by Judas priest.

Old diaries tell us about the vocabulary of coastal Maine people of the past. The language of Jonathan Fisher's journals cannot be regarded as typical of the local language of his time. He was a Harvard graduate. He read Greek, Latin, Hebrew, and French and knew a little Malayan and Indian. *Charles Foster's Journal* (University of Maine, 1975) is a good source of information about the vocabulary of eastern Maine in the 1830s and 1840s. Quite at random, here are a few of his words: jobbing (doing odd chores), dip in an oar (to interfere), how's the body? (how are you?), get my Ebeneazer up (to get angry), to throw a damper (to discourage), the old haymaker (the sun), a rinktum-ditty (a noisy party), garden sass (fresh vegetable), palmy days (prosperous times).

Blue Hillers, like other residents of the coastal area of eastern Maine, have speech habits copied from their grandfathers and great-grandfathers. Professor Raven McDonald of the University of Chicago spent thirty-seven years making a study of the regional speech differences in the United

States. In his *Linguistic Atlas of New England* he pointed out that the people of east coastal Maine have a fondness for contraction: "t'will" for "it will"; "t'wont" for "it won't"; "mor'n" for "more than"; "t'wixt" for "between." Often we substitute "ay-er" for yes; "nope" for no. Our favorite preposition is "up," and we combine it with various verbs: "fix up" meaning to repair or improve; "eat up" meaning to devour; "read up" meaning to study; and "go up" meaning to travel to a place. McDonald noticed that we are loath to say, "I don't know." When asked a question, we often answer, "I'm not sure," or " I do not quite remember."

No one had a keener ear for Maine speech than E. B. White, and no one wrote more kindly about it than he. He wrote that though our talk may not always be a model of good grammar and pronunciation, it is always a pattern of good sense and high interest.

Blue Hill speech has its roots in the past. It is alive and growing. I am proud to speak it.

Rusticators and Summer People

The Homestead, Parker Point, Bluehill, Maine.

Courtesy of Robert Sweetall

9

The Rusticators

FOLKS DOWN EAST are keenly conscious of the nuances of meaning expressed by our English nouns. When a noun fails to give the idea required, they originate new terms. The natives called the first generation of summer visitors "rusticators," and when the word seemed no longer suitable, they substituted the simple expression, "summer people."

Summer visitors have been coming to Penobscot and Blue Hill bays since the last decades of the nineteenth century. The story of the start of the summer business in Blue Hill may be taken as typical.

In 1879 Mr. Hartford Sweet of Salem, Massachusetts, was advised by his doctor to go to the country to live. A friend suggested that he buy a farm in Blue Hill. Mr. Sweet acted upon the suggestion and purchased from Israel Parker his promontory farm washed on three sides by the waters of Blue Hill Bay. Three years later Mr. and Mrs. Sweet advertised for boarders. The good food served at the "Homestead" drew so many boarders that by 1884 the facilities at the farm were overcrowded. Mr. Sweet solved the difficulty by giving a plot of land to Mr. and Mrs. Rogers, his star boarders, who built a cottage but continued to eat at the Sweets'. Soon after, twenty acres of land were sold on the northern side of the farm to two friends who laid out roads and surveyed lots. Within half a dozen years a group of bungalows had been built on Parker's Point, as the promontory came to be called, but all paths led to Mr. Sweet's, for the owners of the bungalows still dined at the Homestead.

While Mr. Sweet was responsible for the start of Blue Hill's summer business, it was George Stover, president of the Blake Pump Company of New York, who became the enthusiastic sponsor of the Blue Hill Inn on a hilltop overlooking the village. This catered to boarders and to dinner guests who lived in cottages and remodeled farmhouses in the vicinity. It was Mr. Stover who was responsible for the establishment of daily steamboat service during the summer months.

Mr. Stover was a one-man publicity bureau long before the days of publicity bureaus. In Maine, New York, and New Jersey papers there appeared glowing descriptions of Mr. Stover's town. The coolness of the climate was a favorite point of emphasis. "During the entire summer the weather is so cool that one may wear an overcoat in July," wrote one newsman. A writer who wished to please all tastes assured the reader, "In Blue Hill one may have a complete rest or may indulge in the most fashionable whirl." The mineral springs, the fairground, and the racing track all received favorable publicity. One optimistic journalist referred to Blue Hill as "a summer resort almost equal to Poland Springs and Saratoga."

Mr. Stover's promotional efforts brought results. By 1908 there were twenty-three "cottages" in the region of Parker's Point, eight in the village, and four on the eastern side of the

Bay. The Blue Hill Inn, the Blue Hill House, and the Pendleton House were booked with paying guests, while Mrs. David Allen at the Salt Pond and Mrs. Wilbur Wardwell at East Blue Hill opened their own homes to "summer boarders," as their contemporaries dubbed them. The people who built their own cottages were called "cottagers." To both, the natives gave the name of "rusticators." The "rusticators" gravely referred to themselves as the "summer colony."

The word *colony*, whether selected by forethought or by chance, was a well-chosen term, for it implied homogeneity. Blue Hill rusticators were indeed homogeneous. They were all people of wealth, many of whom had made their own fortunes. They came chiefly from suburban towns of Massachusetts, New York, New Jersey, and Ohio. Many came from the same locality—not a few were relatives. Love of music was a tie that united them. Wolf Fries was one of the first of a notable group of musicians who came to town.

Bluehill Fair at Mountain Park, Bluehill, Me.

Courtesy of Robert Sweetall

He brought Mrs. Tappan, who in turn was responsible for the coming of Franz Kneisel. Mr. Kneisel influenced Mr. H. E. Krehbiel and Mr. Horatio Parker to join the group. The Sunday afternoon musicales presented by these talented musicians became the high point of the week.

The members of the summer colony also showed taste in the erection of their homes. Rambling bungalows with massive field stone chimneys and wide verandas were built on the rocky points by the bayside. However, some bought old homes and wrought a sad transformation by the addition of towers, porches, and bay windows. Frederick Law Olmsted, the great landscape architect, advised Mr. Benjamin Curtis in the remodeling of the Milford Grindle farmhouse, with the happy result that modern additions did not destroy the beauty of the original proportions.

The rusticators were united in their enthusiasm for Blue Hill. This ardor was especially evident on the day of their arrival for the summer season. Some came by steamer to Rockland where an early morning shift was made to the local steamboat. As the boat, the *Herbert Morrison* or the *Catherine* or the *Boothbay*, edged into the ledge-strewn harbor of the inner bay, excited rusticators strained their eyes for the first glimpse of the home cottage. When its roof was seen through the trees, some child of the family was sent to ask the obliging captain to blow the whistle. In early summer the steamboat's course into the harbor was accompanied by prolonged whistling as cottage after cottage was saluted at the request of the happy owner.

The excitement fairly bubbled over when the boat docked. Firstcomers among the rusticators were joyfully on hand to greet later ones. Familiar native figures called out hearty welcomes. Arthur Herrick, the steamboat agent, and Dan Treworgy and Rob Hinckley, who drove carriages for the village hotels, were there. Coachmen and gardeners were there. Some had driven to the wharf in pony carts, others in carriages, and a few in covered buggies. Mr. Benjamin Curtis was met by his farmer and the oxcart. On the return trip to the Curtis home the farmer and the family occupied the cart while Mr. Curtis, attired in all the dignity of a proper Bostonian, wielded the goad stick.

Enthusiasm held even when the rusticators reached town after a long train trip to Ellsworth and a fourteen-mile buckboard ride. The monotony of the long ride was lightened by sampling the contents of the food hampers that kind neighbors had prepared for them. Weariness and monotony were forgotten when the travelers reached the crest of Greene's Hill and looked down on the village. And there was the bay, scalloped with promontories and dotted with islands.

The arrival was likely to be the most exciting day of the summer, for in spite of the fashionable whirl which Mr. Stover promised, the rusticators led quiet lives. Rocking and swinging must have been major pastimes, for the wide verandas were crowded with rattan rockers. Every lawn had its swing-chair; every cottage orchard, its hammock.

Walking was a favorite recreation. Walkers were of two schools. Some strolled. The strollers always returned laden with spoils: huge bunches of wildflowers, pockets filled with shells, cups of ripe berries. Others hiked. The hikers returned worn out but triumphant, with their tales of distance covered and speed made. But whether a rusticator strolled or hiked, he carried a cane. A cane-holder stood in the hall of every cottage, and a real walking enthusiast had a collection of canes: massive mahogany ones, a few of lithe bamboo, and one or two of polished maple. A host was expected to outfit his guests in the matter of canes if he proposed a leisurely stroll down the lane or gave the challenge for a hike to the top of the mountain.

Rusticators bathed in the salt water. Cubicle bath houses were erected at the water's edge, and one was expected to go to the shore fully clothed, repair to the bath house to change to a bathing suit, and then enter the water immediately. To lie on the beach in bathing attire, either before or after a swim, was a practice forbidden by rusticator mores.

A few rusticators owned rowboats, and after the turn of the century some of the more daring purchased motor launches that were run for them by retired sailors. But it is safe to say most first-generation rusticators never felt at home on the water. They preferred to do their traveling by land and they did a considerable amount of it. Buckboard rides were often organized. Two or three of the long, three-seated wagons were hired from the local livery stable; family carts and carriages were pushed into service so that the number of the party might amount thirty or forty.

Buckboard excursions had favorite destinations: Castine for a picnic on the grass-grown remains of old Fort George; Caterpillar Hill with a songfest at sunset; Newbury Neck for a clambake.

It would be unfair to imply that the rusticator did nothing but listen to music, relax, and play. Some of the men delighted to chop and split the wood for their fireplaces. One Philadelphian, who summered for over thirty years in Blue Hill, raked his long driveway every day from May to October. Irish and Swedish help officiated in kitchens, pantries, and laundries, but rusticator housewives looked after their milk rooms, frequently gathered the vegetables, and tended their own flower borders.

Both master and mistress interested themselves in town

affairs. They founded the Village Improvement Society. Most took time to become acquainted with the natives who were their neighbors. Gradually they ceased to be city people staying in the country. They became a part of the town.

As the years went by, the term "rusticators" was heard less and less often. It no longer described the visitors who spent increasingly long vacations in Blue Hill, people whose fathers and grandfathers had summered in town and who considered that their real roots were in the country town at the head of the bay. The term "summer people" displaced that of "rusticator." When was the change made? At about the time when the Model T displaced the buckboard and the golf club supplanted the walking stick.

10

Blue Hill Inn

THE BLUE HILL INN stood at the top of Tenney Hill, a location that gave a view of the bay and Mount Desert mountains on one side, of forests and Blue Hill Mountain on another.

George Stover, who was a Maine native but had become prosperous in Massachusetts, sponsored the building of the inn. In 1888 he had built a cottage on Peters's Point opposite the harbor entrance. He opened the inn in 1896. A structure one hundred eighty-five feet long and thirty-six feet wide, it was designed by W. R. Emerson, one of the developers of Shingle-style architecture. The builder was Eben Mayo, a local contractor. It had a plant for generating electricity, a laundry, a barber shop, and a limited livery stable.

A yearly booklet advertised the inn. The booklet for 1896 announced "The Blue Hill Inn will open June 20th."

The pictures in the booklet must have whetted a reader's desire to visit "beautiful Blue Hill, where the mountain meets the sea." The cover picture shows the front of the three-story shingled structure with its bulging dormers and extended porches. Three horse-drawn carriages stand near the steps, with drivers and passengers ready for a drive. Guests crowd the porch waiting for the departure. The men wear straw hats and business suits. The hatless ladies wear shirtwaists and skirts, some light and some dark. One lady has an opened parasol. Another picture, with the caption "Waiting for Lunch," shows the ladies wearing straw "sailors" or hats bedecked with flowers, plumes, or ribbon windmills. Both men and the ladies in the picture wear cards pinned to their shoulders. Were the cards name cards or luncheon tickets?

Three pictures in the booklet show views from the inn, one of the village and bay, one of the mountain, and one of Blue Hill Falls. There are views of the interior showing the writing room, the ladies' parlor, the social hall, the office, and the dining room. The picture of the dining room is best. Each of the eleven tables, covered with a long linen cloth, bears a sugar bowl, a vinegar cruet, and a container of napkins—certainly linen. Four waitresses stand on the ready prepared to seat the guests. The booklet has pictures of the mineral spring pavilion at North Blue Hill and the monument to the men lost in the Civil War.

The writer of the booklet gave careful information as to how a guest could reach the inn. He devoted six lines to the land route, by train from New York to Ellsworth by way of the New York, Hartford, and New Haven and the Boston and Maine; from Ellsworth to Blue Hill by coach or carriage. He devoted twenty lines to the joys of traveling by the "magnificent New York Sound Steamboats of the Fall River Line, the splendid Boston and Bangor Steamships and Blue Hill Steamboat Line." He used a complimentary adjective to describe the Blue Hill Line. It is clear that the inn ownership preferred that its guests travel by sea. George Stover was a part owner of the Blue Hill Steamship Company.

This statement in the book is difficult to understand: "The Inn is situated a safe distance from the Bay." Did the writer fear a tidal wave? Did he fear that a guest might fall in the waters of the bay? He referred to the prevailing winds blowing from the mountain over the great pine forests "whose balmy breath brings health to the world-worn and weary." It is a fact, however, that the prevailing wind is often from the southeast off the Bay of Fundy. Such a wind brings fog— damp, salty, and blinding. I cannot accept the statement: "There are no mosquitoes in Blue Hill."

The writer set up standards for the guests of the inn: "The Inn is exclusive in the sense of being intended exclusively for people who know what is good and rejoice to get it. There are no limitations of race or religion in its enrollment of guests; the canons of good breeding and the dictates of refined taste being the only requirement." He concludes on a tender note, "The management refers with pleasure to the ladies and the little ones; It is their comfort above all things which is constantly looked out for."

The last page in the booklet gives a list of "References." There are the names of Eugene Hale of the United States Senate, President Eliot of Harvard University, Mr. George Clough, "the famous Boston architect," and an admiral, among others. To one side of the names is a picture of the bottling department of the Blue Hill Mineral Spring. The inference is that the rich and notable at the inn drank mineral spring water.

Two of my friends, Lila Snow and Hattie Gray, worked at the inn early in the 1920s. In successive summers they were office helpers. They answered the phone, greeted guests, and in longhand dealt with the letters of the manager, Mr. Whittington. By that time, the inn had southern owners who hired black help. Lila recalls that she ate in solemn splendor at a table by herself. She often feasted on fresh salmon, likely caught in the Penobscot River. Hattie on occasion did chamber work and waited on tables when there was a banquet. Lila was paid five dollars a week; Hattie, eight dollars. They recall the friendliness of the guests and their fondness for long walks.

The manager of the inn in 1896 was H. L. Banks. He assured his guests that "the cuisine will be first class, of strictly New England Type." The rates were $10 to $15, single; $18 to $25, double. These were likely weekly rates. He listed the facilities as including "Electric Lights, Long Distance Telephone, Telegraphic Office, Saddle Horses, Excellent Livery."

Guests, some of them famous, all of them rich, came to the inn for three decades. They brought business to town. In time some bought land and built "cottages" on Parker Point. The inn gave business to Merrill and Hinckley's grocery and to Horton's dairy. Andrew Grindle's stables and the Chases' stables furnished the guests with buckboards and buggies. In later years Mr. Grindle's fine cars met the guests when they arrived in Ellsworth.

I enjoy the optimism expressed in the little booklet about the inn. The writer certainly believed that the era of the buckboard and the pavilion, the rusticator and the Gibson Girl was the best of all times. Perhaps it was.

11

Mrs. Kline and the Cottagers

Mrs. Virgil Kline was unlike the other ladies of the Blue Hill summer colony. She was a native, born and raised in Sedgwick. She was the great-great-granddaughter of Joseph Wood, one of the two first settlers of Blue Hill.

Mrs. Kline's maiden name was Effie Ober. As Effie Ober, she achieved success in a field previously occupied by men only. As a young woman she had gone to Boston, where by 1879 she was holding two positions: manager of the Roberts' Agency and secretary of the Williams Lecture Bureau. The agencies found work for singers, readers, and lecturers and, in turn, provided organizations with people who entertained or informed.

The spring of 1879 was a slow time for many of Miss Ober's regular patrons. She decided to help some of the musicians who were out of work. She negotiated with the Boston Theater for the use of its facilities for a month and proposed to put on *H. M. S. Pinafore* for a run of two weeks. She chose the cast for the opera and the musicians for the orchestra with great care. Her show ran for seven weeks and, to the delight of the Boston Theater, it earned between $40,000 and $50,000 from the presentation. When the lady-manager was asked to account for the success of the production, she replied, "We had an ideal group."

Effie Ober decided that opportunity was knocking at her door and severed her connection with both the Roberts' Agency and the Williams Bureau. She formed the Boston Ideal Company and took productions of light opera to other cities. All but one of the original players stayed with her; most of them had been educated in England and Italy.

An old scrapbook filled with programs and newspaper clippings gives evidence of the success of the Ideal Company. For some eight or nine years it produced shows from Omaha to Boston. The home city was Boston but Miss Ober always said, "Next to Boston, St. Paul is our favorite city." Nearly every year the troupe went to New York, Philadelphia, Chicago, Cleveland, and Washington, D. C.

Newsmen stressed that Miss Ober was the first woman in the United States to manage an operatic and dramatic company, and they were charmed by the self-assurance of the petite lady, who remarked, "There are positive advantages for a woman to be in business. I think that a woman can do almost anything that she wishes to do." Newspapers were filled with compliments for both the manager and her company: "Miss Ober is clear-headed, cultured and pleasant. She enjoys intelligent conversation." "The Ideal Opera is very much the best light opera company in the country."

Miss Effie Ober was prosperous as well as popular. She became a summer resident of Blue Hill and built for herself a small cottage on Parker Point, which she called "Petit Mascot." Then, suddenly Miss Ober severed her connection with the management of the company, which she proposed to sell. When questioned as to why she gave up her career, she gave several answers: that she was tired of travel; that it would be impossible to replace a Mr. Whitney who was withdrawing from the troupe; that she wished to enjoy the means that she had earned.

Not long after she gave up her business career, she married Mr. Virgil Kline of Cleveland. Years before, she had met Mr. Kline, who was one of the promoters of music in Cleveland. At the time of the marriage he was a widower with three children. He was older than Effie Ober. Mr. Kline was also one of the lawyers for the Standard Oil Company of Ohio and lawyer of the Teagle family, whose wealth came from oil.

Both she and her husband became summer residents of Blue Hill. She inherited her mother's home on South Street, and she remodeled it. In 1908, Mrs. Kline's sister, Elizabeth Merrill bought a nearby house. A third sister, May Ober, who had been Effie Ober's companion during her business years, lived in the Ober cottage on Parker Point.

Mr. Kline directly increased the size of Blue Hill's summer colony. Both the Teagle family and Colonel Frederick Richards, a commander in World War I, came to town at the insistence of Virgil Kline.

Mr. Kline enjoyed knowing the natives. He loved to go down the bay with South Blue Hill fishermen to catch cod and haddock, and he loved to fish the South Street brooks for trout with his neighbor "Gus" Parker. Sometimes he went with a younger friend, Walter Butler. Mr. Kline built a tennis court for himself and his children. When he learned that Mr. Hargrove, the Baptist minister, played tennis, he invited him to use the court and to use it to instruct the boys of his church in the art of the racquet.

As the years passed, Mrs. Kline became the grand lady of the town. She became the planner and the organizer and the financier of good causes. She provided money to purchase a monument for Joseph Wood. She was one of the founders of the Blue Hill Cemeteries Association. She was also one of the founders of the Blue Hill Historical Society and an enthusiastic worker for the 1908 observance of the town's settlement.

She made the concerns of the summer colony her concerns. In the last decades of the nineteenth century and the first decade of the twentieth century, the residents of the Point were concerned because there was no road between Parker Point and the village. For many years musicians gave concerts for the benefit of a road fund.

Mrs. Kline had her own special project to help the Parker Point road fund. On August 31, 1908, she read a paper at the home of Mr. J. C. Rose, Esquire. She entitled her paper "Blue Hill and Parker Point, Maine." She later had the paper printed in booklet form and sold it for the benefit of the Blue Hill Road Association. The one picture in the book shows

Bluehill, Me., Bridge to Parker Point.

Courtesy of Robert Sweetall

the steamboat off Parker Point with Peters's Point and Blue Hill Mountain in the distance.

The booklet tells us a good deal about Mrs. Kline. It shows that she was proud of her local roots and that she was a careful historian. She took pains to tell which Parker families had lived on the Point. She took pains to locate the Sweet boardinghouse and to name the first rusticators who bought land from Mr. Sweet. She included "A List of Blue Hill Cottagers."

It is a little hard to determine Mrs. Kline's criterion for cottager. Was it wealth? Perhaps so. Was it being born out-of-state? Certainly not. Several cottagers were Blue Hill–born. Was it the type of building in which a person resided? No. Several of the cottagers lived in nineteenth-century homes. Some lived in bungalows. Some lived in newly built mansions. Was it the season of their residence? Yes! In Mrs. Kline's language, anyone who came to town in late June and left in early September was a cottager.

Mrs. Kline gave a list of thirty-six cottager families, one of which included sisters with different names. All names but three are of English or Scotch or Irish origin. Three of the names are names of native Blue Hill families.

Mrs. Kline included the names of the cottages. They prove that the cottagers were an imaginative group. Some of the names tell something about the property: Seven Acres, the Maples, Sunset Rock, Juniper Rock Slide, the Birches. Some have Indian names: Lappahanink, Winne-cowetts. Some have names rooted in the past: the Old Peters Place, the Dodge Farm, the Bushrod Hinckley Homestead. Two had foreign names: Schloss and Fagerheim. The name of the Kline home requires no explanation. It was Ideal Lodge.

12

The Brooks Family Arrives

WHEN I WAS A CHILD, the coming of the Brooks family was the event of the summer, second only to the Fourth of July. Mr. and Mrs. Brooks, son Win, and daughter El lived in East Orange, New Jersey. In 1907 they built a California-style bungalow in the Friend's Corner neighborhood and during the summer lived there in some degree of style.

Mr. Brooks had been a poor boy and he took pride that he had come up in the world. He owned a factory that made seals placed on doors of loaded freight cars. His billfold was always filled with new tens and twenties. When he traveled, he wore a moneybelt under his vest. The belt was filled with one hundred dollar bills. I have this on good authority. He told my father so. He took pride that he was able to help his wife's less prosperous relatives, Aunt Lil and Uncle Bob and Uncle Gordon. He took pride that his bungalow had rooms for Win's Princeton roommate and for El's friends. The guest rooms were never empty.

Mr. Brooks and family journeyed by steamer from New York City to Boston, where they took the "Boston boat" to Rockland. In Rockland they made an early-morning shift to the *Catherine* or the *Boothbay* that brought them to Blue Hill in mid-morning. When the family came, they were met at the wharf by a liveried servant ready to tote the bags and the trunks.

Before the family came late in June, local women cleaned the bungalow and the gardener planted a vegetable garden, set out annuals, and mowed the lawn. Just before his employer arrived, he cleaned the barn, curried the horse, and polished the buggy. He knew that Mr. Brooks was fussy about his possessions and that on his arrival he would give them the closest of inspections.

Our neighbor, Dan Treworgy, became the gardener. He was a retired granite cutter. In tending flowers he was willing but not able, so he had to depend upon my mother's advice. Mrs. Brooks was fond of dahlias and she always had a long row of them growing in front of the porch. Every year she sent a few new tubers. One April she sent a "Calvin Coolidge" root with the message, "Papa wants you to give special attention to this tuber." Dan gave "Coolidge" extra fertilizer and the best place in the sun. But—alas—while the Lady Marys and Dorothy Whites sprouted and grew, there was no sign of growth from Coolidge. At last, in vexation Dan dug up the tuber and found it fat and firm but with no sprout. My father's diagnosis was "Calvin does not choose to grow."

The day before the coming of the Brooks family, Mother had a special task to which she devoted an entire afternoon. She arranged bouquets for the bungalow sitting room, dining room, bedrooms, back porch, and front porch. Only the kitchen was bouquetless. She drafted the children of the neighborhood to pick wildflowers. She asked Cousin Austin to cut cedar for the great baskets that stood either side of the front door. She picked flowers from her own borders. No matter how appetizing the the dinner smells from the kitchen, the fragrance of Mother's bouquets overpowered them. My father was never one to criticize Mother, but he did once remark to me, "The coming of the neighbors gives your mother the chance to go on a real bouquet binge."

Mr. and Mrs. Brooks always called at our home on the evening of the day of their arrival. Both were stout people and unused to any exercise. They walked the short distance from their bungalow to our farmhouse, and they were out of breath when they arrived. Mr. Brooks was glad to hand his cane to Father, and Mrs. Brooks gratefully placed her packages on the table. Embraces were exchanged between the ladies. There was no exchange of news. Nor was there need of such an exchange. Mother and Mrs. Brooks wrote each other twice a month so that we knew all about Win and El and Mrs. Brooks's relatives. Mr. and Mrs. Brooks knew

Bluehill, Maine.

Courtesy of Robert Sweetall

about the work at the granite yard, the neighborhood news, and our relatives.

My chief interest was in the packages on the table. Mrs. Brooks sensed my suspense and soon presented me with a package, sometimes two. She always gave me a summer dress, usually one trimmed with lace or embroidery. One year she gave me a two-way hat that won me the envy of the girls in the village. Worn one side out, it was a blue velvet cap. Turned the other side out, it became a black-and-white checked cap. On both sides there was a slit to hold a long feather. It was just such a cap as Heidi wore when she tended her Swiss goats. The hat still hangs on a nail in the attic though the feather has long since been lost. Once every summer I bring the cap downstairs and wear it for an afternoon stroll.

Mr. Brooks presented no gifts on his arrival but he was an all-summer gift-giver. A crate of oranges or a basket of peaches or a bag of melons or a box of candy might appear at any time on our door-rock. One August he gave the gift of all gifts—a freezer of Mrs. Thurlow's ice cream brought all the way from Rockland on the steamer *Catherine*.

I do not recall that Win and El made an early-summer call on my family. But their presence in the neighborhood enlivened the Corner and their activities were a matter of general interest. Did Win bring tennis racquets and golf clubs? How many girls came with El? Could it be that Win would fall in love with El's friend Nan?

One year the Brookses did not come until the Fourth of July because of an emergency in the family. I was so excited over firecrackers and a picnic and the Brookses' arrival coming on the same day that I ran a fever. Mother was all keyed up over holiday pies and bungalow bouquets, but Father kept calm. He advised: "Just rejoice in the plethora of riches."

13

The Restless Rusticator

OUR NEIGHBOR BENJAMIN CURTIS was a rusticator who never rested. He and Mrs. Curtis with their four children came to Blue Hill early in the twentieth century. For two years they boarded in the Dodge homestead at the village and then they bought two farmhouses in the Friend's Corner neighborhood. The smaller house was used by the gardener, with two rooms reserved for the use of the help. In the gray barn lived two Jersey cows and Star and Bright, the oxen. Mr. Curtis made no changes in this house, but he surrounded it with a handsome granite wall and a line of lilacs.

The larger house underwent some changes. Walls were removed so that three rooms were united to make one large living room, and dormers increased the size of the bedrooms. A porch was built facing the west. No less man than Frederick Law Olmsted gave advice on the side garden, the terrace, the "turn-a-go-round" with its half-circle of shrubs, and the long walk that led to the teahouse and the swimming pool. The lawn in front of the house was separated from the road by posts made of granite blocks, and little evergreens were planted between the posts. All these changes kept Mr. Curtis very busy: he pounded nails, he mixed cement, he planted shrubs. In the great barn near the house lived the little Shetland pony that belonged to his daughters. When all the changes were made, he named his estate Starboard Acres. The family moved in and brought with them maids Lexie and Bessie. Two years later Jane was born and her nursemaid, Mary Marelli, joined the family.

Mr. Curtis and his partner, Mr. Cameron, had a business selling Copley Prints, brown-and-white reproductions of masterpieces. I never knew Mr. Curtis to return to Boston in the summer. It would seem that during the vacation months Mr. Cameron ran the business. There was enough to do on his estate to keep Mr. Curtis busy. He drove the oxen, weeded the garden, and gathered the produce. He went to the woods and selected the trees to be cut. When he was not busy with outside chores he busied himself indoors. He played the piano, read the Boston papers and the art magazines, and read German and French novels. He made an old shop near the kitchen into an office and there he wrote letters and summoned his children for consultations.

Mr. Curtis was one who expected much of his children. He expected them to be handsome, talented, quick to learn, and energetic. Gordon and Robert were the oldest and they were handsome lads, but showed no talent for either languages or music. They were energetic but not along the lines that their father approved. The oldest daughter, Carol, won approval from her father for her energy and her effort. But Helen was his pride. She was beautiful, musical, quick to learn, and as energetic as her older sister. Mr. Curtis had no expectations for Jane, who was much younger than the other children. He considered that at birth she had reached perfection. The rules laid down for the other children did not apply to little Janey. She played chopsticks on her father's cherished piano, and she and I made mud pies on his office floor. When we played church we used his best hat as the contribution box.

The affairs of Starboard Acres and the management of his children did not consume all of Mr. Curtis's energy and organizational skills. He did not own a boat, but once or twice a summer he borrowed the launch of his brother-in-law, E. J. Brooks. Mr. Brooks was glad to loan his boat, but his captain, Homer Clark, was not pleased to be loaned. Homer never took out a Curtis party that a wrangle did not ensue. One year Mr. Curtis invited more guests than the boat could take. The captain insisted upon a "count-out," and some of the guests trudged home disappointed. Another year Mr. Curtis and another man chose to ride in the dory towed by the launch. The captain had to speak hot words before the two Bostonians came into the big boat.

Mr. Curtis had better luck with his buckboard rides to Caterpillar Hill. He hired two or three buckboards, each pulled by two horses. Blue Hill buckboards had three or four bench seats, but a friend well versed in horse-drawn vehicles has assured me that large resort towns had buckboards with five or six seats that were drawn by four horses. Jane and I liked to sit on the front steps and watch Mr. and Mrs. Curtis and their guests board the buckboards. Children were not invited. Our mouths watered at the sight of the hampers. We had watched Bessie and Lexie pack the luncheon, and we knew that the hampers held ham sandwiches, stuffed eggs, apple turnovers, and chocolate brownies. The expedition always left late in the afternoon. Jane and I did not see the return. It was long after our early bedtime.

For all the children of the neighbors, Mr. Curtis planned hayrack rides. The gardener filled the rack half full of hay, and we piled aboard with shouts of pleasure. The nursemaid went along to watch over Janey, Mr. Curtis drove the oxen, and Gordon and Robert followed the rack on their bicycles. We went to a cove at East Blue Hill where Mr. Curtis and his sons dug clams, made a fire, and prepared a bed of seaweed on which to steam the clams. About the time the clams were done, Mrs. Curtis and Carol drove up in the pony cart, which was well packed with bottles of lemonade and boxes of sandwiches.

Mr. Curtis's best-remembered expedition was the swamp jaunt that he planned for four friends who lived on Beacon Hill. One of the men was associated with the *Atlantic Monthly*. The day before the trip, Mr. Curtis and his boys made careful preparations. They unpinned the body of the dump cart, tilted it back and carefully washed it. Then they leveled the body and repinned it, oiled the wheels and polished the goad stick. Rather against his wishes, Robert brushed off Star and Bright, the oxen.

When the morning for the trip came, Mrs. Curtis excused herself from going, but she was on hand to watch her friends depart. The men wore white duck trousers and carried canes, and the ladies wore pink and blue gowns of linen and lace and carried parasols. They used a stepladder to board the cart. The maids and we children saw them off. Mr. Curtis walked beside the oxen, while Robert was the unwilling guard who brought up the rear of the procession. Mrs. Curtis's farewell words were: "We'll expect you in time for lunch.

But the expedition returned long before lunch. Jane and I were on the front lawn and witnessed the return. The men were hatless and caneless. The parasols of the ladies were bent and soiled. Summer gowns and duck trousers were covered with swamp muck. Their wearers were "down at the mouth." Mr. Curtis was more so. Only Robert was cheerful.

It was Robert who later gave an account of what had happened. Way in the woods in the middle of the big swamp, the pin came out, the cart dumped, and in a flurry of parasols, canes, hats, and folding chairs the cart passengers slid into the mire. Robert's comment was: "It was as good as a circus. The women screamed, and the men swore, and the *Atlantic Monthly* chap used some words that I never heard before."

One July Mr. Curtis suggested that he and the boys provide a surprise for Janey's birthday party. When Mrs. Curtis asked that she be let in on the secret, Mr. Curtis said: "A surprise known by four people is no surprise. Wait and see."

The day of the party was fair and sunny. The party went off well. Some ten little girls were guests. All were dressed in white dresses with sashes and hair ribbons to match and each brought Jane a gift.

Soon Mr. Curtis arrived with the announcement: "Now, children, the time for the big surprise is at hand!" He produced a long length of ribbon and bade the children to form a line. Each child grasped the ribbon. Mr. Curtis ordered: "Helen is to walk at the end of the line and Mary may walk beside Janey at the head of the line right behind me. You 'grown-ups' stay on the porch."

Off we marched with Mr. Curtis beating a drum. We went into a small orchard at the edge of the field. Beyond it were the woods. Suddenly from the woods there burst two Indians (Gordon and Robert) wearing feathered headdresses and swinging hatchets. The whoops that they uttered were ear-splitting.

The line of screaming little girls broke. We started to run.

Some fell, and others stumbled over them. Mrs. Curtis, Carol, Bessie, and Lexie ran toward us. Helen and Mary joined the rescue party. Soon each child was in someone's arms. One child was hysterical and kicked her rescuer in the face. Never did a birthday party end with such a finale. Mrs. Curtis saw to it that her husband provided no further "surprises" for Jane's parties.

My father and mother liked Mr. Curtis very much indeed. They often spoke of his energy. Mother used to say: "Our neighbor plans well." Father was more specific: "Mr. Curtis does more than plan. He expedites expeditions. He supplies surprises."

14

Gentle Philadelphians

MOST OF THE BLUE HILL SUMMER PEOPLE were first- or second-generation millionaires. We natives were always curious about the source of their wealth: whether oil or steel, refrigerators or railroad-car seals, shoe blacking or whiskey, railroads or stores, mills or mines.

The Owen family was distinctive. The family's moderate wealth dated way back into the early nineteenth century. The Owens had lived on Philadelphia's Chestnut Street for generations.

There were three Owen sisters and one brother who came to Blue Hill. All were single, though rumor had it that David had once been married. The sisters were Elizabeth, Mary, and Caroline, but they were always called Sister Bessie, Sister Minnie, and Sister Carrie. Carrie was the youngest; she had a bad back and was an invalid. There was a rumor that one of her sisters had dropped her when she was a baby.

The father of the family had been a Union general in the Civil War and had commanded troops at Second Bull Run.

He founded and edited a law journal. The two older sisters owned and managed a Philadelphia tea shop, the Green Dragon. Brother David had no visible means of support. He was kept busy following the directions given him by his sisters.

Early in this century the sisters and their brother built a summer home on a seaboard cliff between Friend's Corner and the Head-of-the-Bay. They lived in some style with a cook, a second girl, and a chauffeur, all "native help." I use an expression of half a century ago. No Maine native will consent to be called a servant. The Owen cottage was an eighth of a mile from the main road. In coastal Maine talk a cottage is a dwelling occupied for the summer months only. It may have four rooms or sixty-four rooms.

After a time the Owens had a second cottage. They bought the old office of a granite company, enlarged it, painted it pink, called it Larkspur Lodge, and opened a teahouse in it. Sister Minnie presided over the tea arrangements. Sister Bessie sold goods imported from Europe and the Orient. Sister Carrie was too frail to help. Brother David daily raked the graveled road between Larkspur Lodge and the big cottage, Tyn-y-coed.

Brother David was a short, broad-shouldered man. His face was round and red, his teeth very white, and his eyes sharp and merry. He loved to tell a story. He always concluded the story with the remark, "I have to laugh." Then he did laugh. He sang tenor in the choir of the Congregational Church. I again quote rumor: he was once an opera singer. Local rumor was very busy with the pre–Blue Hill lives of the newcomers. The glamor of the summer people has long since worn off. Rumor today seldom touches them.

The sisters, all rather short women with black hair, dressed beautifully, and each had a special color for her wardrobe.

Miss Bessie's was purple; Miss Minnie's, green; Miss Carrie's, blue. The shades of blue and green and purple differed from light to dark; a dress might be flowered with other colors; a coat might have a black velvet collar. But never did a sister forget herself and use the color of another sister.

Once when I was a very small child, little Janey Curtis asked me to go for a picnic on the beach at the old paving wharf. Her parents asked the Owens to come as their guests. I went early with the Curtises to the picnic site. The cloth was spread on a flat rock, the lunch baskets were unpacked, and potatoes were baking in the coals of the driftwood fire when the guests of honor arrived. Their chauffeur drove them in the car until a fence barred the road. Then they got out of the car and walked down the field to the beach. Brother David came first, swinging his cane and shouting, "I've got a story to tell you." He was followed by his sisters who walked in single file according to age. Miss Bessie wore a purple linen dress; Miss Minnie, a green one; Miss Carrie, a blue one. Each carried an open parasol that matched her dress. The chauffeur walked at the end of the procession. He carried three cushions; a purple one for Miss Bessie, a green one for Miss Minnie, and a blue one for Miss Carrie.

After the picnickers finished their lunch of sandwiches and baked clams, we children went to the beach where we skipped rocks, searched for shells, and waded in the water. When we tired of the beach, we went to the meadow to gather wildflowers and made three bouquets: one of purple asters for Miss Bessie, one of ferns for Miss Minnie, and sprays of blue chicory for Miss Carrie. We children took care to observe the rules of the Owen color code.

15

Broken Friendship

THE STREAM OF OLD FRIENDSHIP did not always run smoothly with our first-generation summer families.

The Curtis and the Loring families were close friends as long as they lived in Wellesley Hills, Massachusetts. Mr. Curtis went to Boston five days a week. Mrs. Curtis stayed at home with her two sons and two daughters and the three servants. Mr. Loring was a prosperous lawyer who also went to his office five days a week. Mrs. Loring stayed at home with her two sons and their one servant. One summer, the Curtis family boarded at the Dodge homestead in Blue Hill Village. In their second summer in Maine they bought a half-mile of shore property and two farmhouses east of the village. In the summer of 1905 or 1906, the Curtises moved to their country estate and lived there in some degree of style. In 1907 little Janey was born on an ancestral bed moved from Wellesley Hills.

The Lorings bought their Blue Hill summer home in 1907. They bought less land than the Curtises, but their house was far superior to either of the Curtis farmhouses. They bought a granite house, originally built as a store and a boardinghouse for the quarrymen and cutters who worked at the Doorstone quarry. To their home they added dormers, porches, and a zigzag ell that zagged to avoid a huge boulder. The ell included rooms for two maids, but the family never had but one—a maid of all chores.

My Great-aunt Fan lived next door to the Lorings. It was a matter of pride to her that her neighbor was an author. By 1907 Mrs. Loring had written both articles and novels. It was not surprising that she had a writing career. She was the daughter of Walter Baker, who published plays, and the sister of a man who produced one of the early comic strips.

Mrs. Loring's books helped the family finances and added to the family prestige. When the Owens, an old Philadelphian family, built a house nearby, they made much of the Lorings. When the Brooks family built a home near the Curtis place, it was with no little pride that Sister Mary said to Sister Josie, "Emilie Loring, the novelist, is my dear friend."

Alas! The close friendship between the two Wellesley Hills families, the Curtises and the Lorings, did not last. Three incidents destroyed it.

It was unfortunate that Mr. Curtis's western acres abutted Mr. Loring's eastern acres. There soon arose a misunderstanding over the map provided by the surveyor. The two neighbors appealed to a local surveyor and an Ellsworth lawyer, and both of the impartial parties agreed with Mr. Loring's interpretation of the map. Mr. Loring was jubilant; Mr. Curtis was crestfallen. Their ladies took no part in the land dispute. "Dear Emilie" and "Dear Mary" continued to see each other nearly every day.

Early the following summer, there was an unfortunate incident at the Loring dining table. Mr. and Mrs. Curtis were there with their older son, Gordon, as were the four Owens and Mr. and Mrs. Brooks and daughter Elinor. Young Robert Loring was also among the diners. Mrs. Curtis's Lexie and Bessie were in the kitchen to help with the preparation and the serving of the meal.

When the Lorings and their guests came to the table, Mr. Brooks noticed that thirteen people were about to dine. He said nothing at the time but he later remarked to his wife, "Just the minute I tucked the corner of the dinner napkin inside my vest, I said to myself, 'There is sure to be trouble.'"

And trouble there was! The first course was served with decorum and eaten with relish. While the dishes were being removed, there was a lull in the general conversation. Mr. Curtis took the opportunity to ask Mr. Loring a question. Mr. Curtis, art critic and music lover, had a keen sense of humor and loved jokes. Mr. Loring, the dignified lawyer, had little use for such.

Said the art critic to the lawyer, "Mr. Loring, as a lawyer, give me the answer to this question: Can a man marry his widow's sister?"

Eleven listeners caught the catch in the query, but not the lawyer. His quick reply was, "Certainly, Mr. Curtis, he can."

The answer brought a ripple of laughter from the gentle Philadelphians. Mrs. Loring exclaimed, "Oh, Victor!" Mrs. Curtis and Mrs. Brooks and Elinor smiled. But it was Mr. Brooks and the two boys at the table who caused the great commotion. Mr. Brook's shouts of laughter were heard in the kitchen. The scion of the Curtis family beat his dessert spoon on the table and young Loring so forgot himself that he stamped his feet on the floor.

Mr. Loring at once saw his error. He was humiliated. He was angry. He pushed back his chair, threw his dinner napkin on the table, and stomped upstairs.

It was Mrs. Loring who brought order from the confusion. She quelled the boys with a look. She rang the bell, and when Lexie appeared, she said, "We'll have our dessert and coffee in the living room, please." She quietly whispered to her son, "Go upstairs and ask your father to come down."

Some time later Mr. Loring returned to the fold, but he was a silent host.

The crowning blow came at the close of the summer when Mrs. Loring gave a tea party. She invited not only the summer people who lived near her but she also invited the Slavens, the Boardmans, the Millikens, and some friends from Parker Point. In fact, she asked so many guests that there was a scarcity of cups and saucers. She was forced to use her grandmother's old ivory cups and saucers. She said to the maid, "Do be careful when you wash them."

The maid was careful but not careful enough to notice that one cup had a cracked handle. It was Mary Curtis's ill fortune to have that cup. When she raised the tea-filled cup to her lips, the handle separated from the cup. The cup dropped to her lap and the hot tea made a puddle on the new gown that her husband had bought her on a recent trip to London.

There was consternation. Mrs. Loring ran with tea napkins in her hand to dry "Dear Mary's" skirt. Sister Josie cried out, "Is Mary burned?" Both Mr. Loring and Mr. Curtis rushed to the scene of the mishap.

Said the mortified host, "I'll buy Mary a new gown."

Snapped back the angry Curtis, "You will do no such thing. I can well afford to buy gowns for Mary. But in the future I shall see to it that my wife does not frequent homes where guests are given cracked cups."

That incident ended the Loring-Curtis friendship—though both Emilie and Mary longed for a reconciliation.

Both Aunt Fan and Mother liked to discuss the disastrous tea party. Aunt Fan felt that Mr. Curtis had been too quick to take offense. Mother felt that the Curtises were blameless.

Father never joined the discussion, but he sometimes interrupted with a comment: "Everyone has heard of a tempest in a teapot. But whoever heard of a quarrel over a teacup? A cracked one, at that!"

16

Summer People at Play

THE SUMMER PEOPLE who lived in or near Friend's Corner were a fun-loving group. They knew how to enjoy themselves whether on sea or on shore.

The Slavens had a steam yacht, the *Alfredine IV*. Mr. Brooks had a good-sized motorboat, locally called the "Brooks launch." My father had small regard for the craft. He used to remark, "It is top-heavy and likely to roll over when a swell hits it. It is not seaworthy the other side of Long Island."

The Owens had a rowboat that they used for trips to the country club and the Head-of-the-Bay. Mr. Curtis did not own a boat and he took pains to declare, "I prefer to keep my feet on terra firma."

There were then few sailboats in Blue Hill Bay. Dr. Seth Milliken owned one, named the *Thistle*. There was a Friendship sloop for hire at the Falls. It was probably owned by Captain Albert Conary. "Tad" Kline owned another, the *Indra*. The Haskells' *Troubador* graced the inner harbor.

Every cottager provided for recreation at home. The Owens had a sunken garden. Mr. Curtis furnished a pony and a swimming pool for his five children. The Slavens had a tennis court and wide porches and terraces for resting and reading. Mr. Brooks made ample provision for Mr. Win and Miss Elinor. In the basement of the cottage was a billiard table and between the house and the lower field was a tennis court. Across the road was a miniature golf course in the center of which was a mound some five feet long and three feet high. The children of the neighborhood liked to watch Win and his friends try to knock balls over the obstacle.

Both Win and Elinor always had a friend in residence. I have a recollection of Win's friends, their long legs clad in white duck trousers. Elinor's friends, Nan Baldwin and Dorothy Seaburger, I remember well. They played games with the little girls of the Corner, they made fudge for us, they took us rowing.

Bluehill, taken from Parker Point Wharf, Bluehill, Maine.

Courtesy of Robert Sweetall

My neighbors gave teas. Each hostess had a tea party specialty. Mrs. Slaven's was macaroons. Mrs. Brooks's was sour cream cookies made by her Swedish cook. Mrs. Curtis's was brownies and she made them herself. The Owen sisters served sliver-thin sandwiches with a filling of nasturtium leaves.

Mrs. Curtis had the most lavish provision for giving teas. The teahouse, well below the house on the other side of the road, was built of paving stones with a stone floor and open sides. It was furnished with wooden chairs and tables that were made locally. It had a corner cupboard filled with blue Italian pottery that showed pictures of the Curtis house. Beside the teahouse was a walled-up spring; below it was the swimming pool.

A sloping walk led from the road to the teahouse. Here and there a steep incline was covered with steps of cut granite. Shrubs and small pines lined the walk. The walk had an elegant beginning in what we children called the "turn-a-go-round." It was a drive in the shape of a half-circle and around it grew hardy roses and shrubs. In the center were more roses and a brass sundial set on a paving-stone base. No one entertained at tea more graciously and more stylishly than did Mrs. Curtis.

Sometimes my neighbors took tea at the country club across the bay.

Before the day of the family automobile, going to the club took time. They went by boat or by horse and carriage. Mr. Curtis once caused a mild sensation at the club by arriving in a dump cart drawn by his oxen, Broad and Star.

One of my friends has told me a story about his taking the Owens for tea at the club. At the time he was fourteen years old. He did chores for the Owen family and became the devoted follower of Brother David. When the tide was just right and the bay was dead calm, he rowed them to the clubhouse. He had a mission other than rowing, and only he and David Owen knew about the second mission. He carried in his pocket Mr. Owen's pipe and tobacco pouch. When the family was well settled in the boat, one of the sisters was sure to say, "David, I hope you left that horrid pipe at home."

Brother David's reply was swift and truthful. "Not a thing in my pockets but my handkerchief and my change purse."

Once the boat reached the clubhouse float, once the Owens went ashore, the boy tied up the boat and walked to the clubhouse. Before he joined the other boys who had rowed their employers to tea, he went to the back of the clubhouse. There on a shelf back of a gutter he left Brother David's pipe and tobacco pouch. At least once in the afternoon Mr. Owen came out of the clubhouse for a breath of air and a secret smoke. When there were signs that the party was ending, David's young friend sauntered back of the clubhouse and retrieved his employer's possessions.

I had no part in my neighbor's tea parties, but I was a joyful participant in their birthday parties. Mrs. Slaven always had a party for one of her grandchildren. Mrs. Brooks entertained to honor little Virgina Chase, a village child whom she loved. Mrs. Curtis always had a party for Jane on the child's birthday. Mrs. Thurlow's ices were served at all. This ice cream, famous for richness and flavor, came from Rockland on the steamboat. There were always two gallons, one of vanilla and one of chocolate.

I remember a birthday party for Miss Elinor Brooks. It was given by adults and planned as a surprise party. Mr. Curtis was the master of ceremonies. He had directed that each guest should appear in costume at three o'clock at the

Wood barn, from which they would march to the Brooks cottage. Mrs. Loring, the author of popular romances, had the most amusing costume. Her shawl was a bedspread and her hat a wicker lampshade. Mr. Curtis assembled his marchers. He and the Curtis sons marched at the head of the column beating drums; Jane and I, beating tin pans, walked at the end of the procession.

Miss Elinor was indeed surprised but so were Mr. Curtis and his marchers. The route of the march was beside our pasture where grazed our family cow and our horse, Prince. The cow was unperturbed by the costumed procession and the beating of drums and pans, but not Prince. He jumped over the fence and entered into the spirit of the occasion. He raced from one end of the line to the other. He whickered, his mane blew in the wind. Timid ladies screamed. Mrs. Loring's "hat" blew off and Prince trampled it. The guests reached the Brooks cottage in sad disarray. Once they went onto the porch, Prince's excitement ebbed and he gave attention to the clover on the lawn. When the guests went into the house for ice cream and cake, he approached the flower garden and ate Mr. Brooks's red dahlias that had been earmarked for display at the Blue Hill fair.

When the party was over, there was no beating of drums and fluttering of flags. The guests were tired. Gordon Curtis carried little Janey, and I was helped along by Janey's older sisters. Mr. Curtis made no attempt to direct the return of the troop to the Wood barn. But Prince was in fine fettle. He jogged briskly along with the party-goers and now and then softly nickered as though to say, "It's great to watch the summer people at play."

17

The Renters

SOME FIFTY YEARS AGO there were five houses in my neighborhood that were rented during July and August. We natives called the occupants of the houses "the renters." We reserved the term "summer people" for the well-settled families who in the 1890s and early years of this century bought shore property, built cottages, and settled in for a lifetime of summer residence in Blue Hill.

The first renters whom I remember were Dr. and Mrs. Abbott, who had been missionaries to India. Their arrival forced me to revise my views about missionaries. I had been brought up to believe that missionaries were poverty-stricken and that their wardrobe came from barrels sent to the missions by American churches. Dr. and Mrs. Abbott arrived in Ellsworth via the Bar Harbor Express. The maids and chauffeur came in the family car, a limousine. We did not know the source of the Abbott wealth. Father had a practical explanation. He said: "Likely either Dr. or Mrs. Abbott had a rich uncle who died and left them a fortune."

I liked my explanation better: Dr. Abbott converted a rich Indian mogul. The prince was so grateful that he presented the Abbotts with a bag of diamonds, garnets, rubies, and emeralds.

The source of their wealth was not the only mystery about the Abbotts. We wondered how Dr. Abbott could have had success converting the Indians. He was a silent and forbidding man. Twelve hours of the twenty-four he kept a roaring fire in the fireplace. He took a late-afternoon walk, his one expedition of the day. He walked with his eyes straight ahead, equally indifferent to the blossoming flowers and the billowing clouds. Mrs. Abbott was very different. Probably it was she who converted the natives. She called on the neighbors and often brought little gifts. I still cherish the tiny gold-embossed tray that she gave Mother. I chose to believe that the tray was given to Mrs. Abbott by an Indian prince—the same one who gave the bag of jewels.

She was a walker, and she usually went to walk taking a spade and a pail. She was a fern enthusiast and came home with fern roots and fronds that she planted in the shady corners of the house. It was the chauffeur's task to water the ferns, and he had plenty of time for this chore because the car was taken from the garage only once a week. One clump of Mrs. Abbott's ferns, planted near the spring, still lives: a green memorial to the lady missionary.

Whenever I think of Dr. and Mrs. Abbott, I recall the line of an old missionary hymn: "From Greenland's icy mountain to India's coral strand." The doctor was the "icy mountain"; his lovely lady, the "coral strand."

The renters who lived in the house near the Abbotts' were a family unit, the Streeters. The father was usually away in the city, maybe counting his money and making more; his beautiful blonde wife played tennis and golf, swam and sailed and walked. Three handsome sons were as athletic as their mother. I never walked by their house that the mother and one of the sons did not rush out to greet me. When they drove by my home, they waved and called out a greeting. The little girl, tended by a nursemaid, usually left the greeting and waving to her mother and brothers.

One summer afternoon I was responsible for a horrendous incident that involved the little girl. Mrs. Streeter was entertaining her tennis group; her sons had taken the cars to go mountain climbing. She phoned in haste to ask if I would bring her over a bottle of cream. I was soon on my way with a gleaming bottle in my hand. As I entered the Streeter yard, I noticed huge black clouds rolling in from the southeast. I looked up and saw the nursemaid and little girl standing beside a bedroom window. The maid spoke to me and the child waved. I returned the greeting by clearly and loudly saying: "See those dark clouds making up in the south? Watch out for a bad blow."

PARKER POINT
BLUEHILL, MAINE.

Courtesy of Robert Sweetall

The response to my mini-weather warning was instant hysterics—the kind without laughter. There came from the little girl such shrieks and wails as I had never heard. I was unnerved. It was fortunate that the cook rushed from the kitchen and took the jar of cream from my trembling hand. It was then that Mrs. Streeter appeared, the very picture of calmness and self-possession in her party gown, her jewels, and high heels. Putting her arm around me, she said: "My dear, you were not to blame. How were you to know that my little girl has an unreasonable fear of wind? She was once caught in a tornado."

The coming of World War II ended the visits of the Streeter family to our neighborhood. I am sure that the three sons fought bravely in the war. I know that Mrs. Streeter headed up one of the women's branches of the armed service. Her physical fitness, calmness, self-assurance, and kindness well fitted her for such a position. I would have trusted her with the command of the Normandy invasion.

The renter who meant the most to me was Mrs. White, an elderly widow who was a member of an old Virginia family. She used to remark: "My mother was one of the most beautiful women in Virginia — my father was one of the ugliest men. Every one of their nine children inherited my father's nose. Just look at mine!" Mrs. White's husband had been in the foreign service; she had lived in many European cities. She used to say: "I'd just get a garden growing well when we would get a new post, and I would have to leave my flowers."

Mrs. White did not garden when she was our neighbor, but she loved to pay morning calls to our garden. I placed a chair for her beside a flower border, and she would sit and look and think and sometimes nap. A single flower always interested her more than an expanse. Her highest praise for a blossom was "It is a poem."

Nearly every week she paid us an evening house call, bringing with her a basket of books and magazines. With Mother, she talked about gardens; with Father, she talked about politics; with me, she talked about novels. It was she who introduced me to Galsworthy and H. G. Wells.

Rachel presided in Mrs. White's kitchen. She ordered the groceries, planned the meals, and advised Mrs. White about the details of daily living. Often it was Rachel who made the important household decisions. Rachel had left Ireland when she was a young girl, and she retained her "old country" accent. She had worked up from "second girl" to cook. She was stout and smiling and kind.

Rachel loved to feed people. For several summers she fed Oscar, a teenager who came once a week to mow the lawn, weed the borders, and do odd chores. He brought his dinner in a lard pail, but Rachel supplemented his fare with rich offerings from her kitchen.

Mrs. White seldom spoke to Rachel about the menu, but one August she was moved to do so. "Rachel," she said, "please don't think I am finding fault. You do a wonderful job planning our meals. I do like coffee pie. I like it very much. But is there any reason why we should have it every week?"

"There is reason and enough!" exclaimed Rachel. "Coffee is Oscar's favorite kind of pie."

After two or three decades the five homes occupied by the renters underwent change. Alas, one burned. The son of the owner took over one of them. Two retired teachers bought a third. Two were bought by renters who, by the process of purchase, became summer people.

18

The Help

THE EARLY BLUE HILL RUSTICATORS seldom had servants. They ate at local boardinghouses. After they built their cottages, they continued to eat at Sweet's or Dodge's. Only now and then did a guest at the Blue Hill Inn have a coachman or chauffeur or a secretary.

In the early decades of this century, when people of wealth started building large cottages in town, they brought in cooks and waitresses, parlor maids and laundresses, nursemaids and governesses. They hired local people as coachmen, chauffeurs, teamsters, gardeners, captains, and day laborers. They called them all servants. The natives called them "the help."

Most of the people on Parker Point had Negro help. By the 1920s, black servants were so numerous in town that they held an "Owls" Ball annually, sometimes at the pavilion on the grounds of the Mineral Spring, sometimes at the town hall. An out-of-town orchestra was hired. Black servants from Mount Desert came to the ball and so did fun-loving Blue Hill natives. The ball was one of the big events of the summer.

Regrettably, the natives called the blacks "coons," but they liked them all the same. The children liked the chauffeurs best and they crowded around them at the post office. Bill Jackson, a stout man in his sixties whose hair was still black, was the favorite of the village boys. Jackson drove for Dr. Dohme and he came alone for the mail. When he saw a child on the road, he stopped the car and took him in. If he was not going in the direction the child was going, he turned the car around and took the child to his destination. Caddies, going to or from the golf club, came to depend upon William for a lift.

Our Friend's Corner summer people had white help. I can recall only two black servants who worked in the neighborhood. One was a stout lady who cooked for one of the renters. One day when I delivered a pint of cream, I saw her beating a cake with her hand in the batter. On a later day she gave me a piece of cake. It tasted all the better for being hand-beaten.

The second black servant whom I recall was a lady who cooked for Miss Littel and Miss Singleton, retired teachers who in the late 1930s bought the Curtis home. The black lady had for years cooked in the home of a Mr. and Mrs. Dobbins of Baltimore. By the 1940s Mr. and Mrs. Dobbins and their three daughters had died. The colored lady kindly consented to come to Blue Hill for the summer as cook for the teachers. She loved the quiet neighborhood and the cool weather. The roasts she baked, the breads she stirred up, and the chowders she made were the talk of all the guests whom the teachers entertained.

On the matter of desserts, though, there was a problem. The teachers liked desserts that were fancy and sweet and highly flavored. They liked a three-layer cake filled with inch-deep frosting. When they asked the visiting cook for such a cake, she said, "I'll make you one jes' like I made for the Dobbinses—two layers, dusted with powdered sugar." The teachers liked a four-egg lemon pie with a meringue, high and swirled. When they requested such a pie, the cook replied, "The Dobbinses never had lemon pie. I'll make you a nice lemon Jell-o, jes' like I made them." The teachers were grateful that the former Baltimore cook came to Maine with them. But they were regretful that she cooked only Dobbins desserts.

The best loved of all the maids who came to Friend's Corner was Mary Morelli, an Italian girl who was Jane Curtis's nursemaid. When Jane grew too old to have a nursemaid, Mary became the second girl. In time she was the only maid that Mr. and Mrs. Curtis had. She was more than maid to Mrs. Curtis. She was advisor, confidant, and friend. One summer Mary's younger sister came to Blue Hill with Mary. The sister lived in Boston and was a devout Catholic. She was older than I. Her talk opened our eyes to a wider world than Blue Hill.

Mrs. Brooks preferred Swedish maids. She said, "They're better cooks than the Irish and neater than the Negroes." Mrs. Brooks's opinions may have been wrong. But this I know: her Swedish girls were fine cooks and neater than wax. Mrs. Brooks chose to do some of the dairy work. Every morning and every night, the cook strained the milk brought warm from the cow. But it was Mrs. Brooks who every mid-morning skimmed the cream from the milk set the night before. The second girl turned the churn but Mrs. Brooks did up the butter.

Hilda, a Swedish maid, served Mrs. Brooks during the years of the First World War. Mrs. Brooks hired her at an employment agency. Hilda was a recent immigrant from her homeland. Mrs. Brooks expected that the maid would know nothing about setting a table and serving. The maid knew all about both. Mrs. Brooks expected that the maid would speak English haltingly. She spoke it fluently, and she also spoke German and French. She could play classical music.

Hilda was as pretty as she was talented. Mr. Brooks used to say, "No matter whom we have for guests, the prettiest woman in our dining room is Hilda." Mrs. Brooks used to add, "And the most talented."

The Swedish girl stayed with the Brooks family for two years. When Miss Elinor, the daughter, left to work in a war canteen in 1916, Hilda sat with Mrs. Brooks in the afternoon and read to her and talked with her. In the evening she played the piano. Some evenings she accepted Mr. Brooks's challenge to a game of checkers.

When the war ended, Hilda went home to Sweden. She and Mrs. Brooks exchanged letters. In a few years Hilda wrote of her wedding and in later years of the birth of children. After Mrs. Brooks died, Miss Elinor and Hilda exchanged letters. In the late 1930s Miss Elinor went to Europe and, at Hilda's invitation, she traveled to Sweden to visit the former servant. Hilda and her husband met Elinor at the station and guided her to the family limousine, chauffeur-driven. They drove to a great estate in the country where there were a housekeeper, a cook, numerous maids, nursemaids, and governesses.

Elinor Brooks was amazed. When she and Hilda were alone, she demanded of Hilda, "Why did you not tell Mother what a good marriage you had made?"

Answered Hilda, "Your mother and I enjoyed the relationship of mistress and maid. It might have spoiled her happy memories of me, had she known that I had become a mistress."

With the passing of the years, local women became cooks for the summer people. Their daughters and nieces became waitresses and chambermaids. The monotony of the summer work was broken by having an afternoon off when the chauffeur drove the help to Ellsworth or Castine. Once every summer, the help on Parker Point had a picnic on the rocks. Some summers, the owner of a yacht would invite all the help to take a trip around Long Island.

Some local women who cooked for the summer people spent a lifetime of summers in the same kitchen. With the passing of the seasons, the mistress often became more and more dependent upon the native cook. Mistress and maid became close friends. Sometimes the latter became the decision-maker of the household.

Some men who did outside work for the summer people spent a lifetime with the same family. Herman Gray started working for the Slavens when he was a boy. He began as coachman, then became the chauffeur, and finally became the jack-of-all-work on the Slaven estate. He knew four generations of the Slaven family. In his last years of working for them, he used to say with a laugh, "When I take Miss Nila and her friends for a little trip in the launch, not one of us is less than seventy-five years old."

19

The Musicians

"Music comes floating to you out of cottage after cottage; it comes from the water; it ebbs out of shady coves and echoes out of dense forests, from voice, from piano, from violin, from cello. Well may the hermit thrush, skillful master of lovely song who from time immemorial has held sway in the pine forest, look to his laurels." Thus did Theodore Nevin of the *Pittsburgh Dispatch* describe Parker Point of the early twentieth century.

Enthusiasm was Mr. Nevin's real name. He wrote of the townspeople of Blue Hill: "They are the real Maine people and are intelligent, educated, and appreciative — they pour out en masse for the concerts, from the village blacksmith, who is a real artist in his trade, to the merchant and the professional man." Nevin wrote of the summer colony: "They are, all in all, an industrious, jovial, genial, gemütlich group of people. I doubt if there is any such gathering anywhere else in the country."

Mr. Nevin was correct when he wrote that Blue Hill natives enjoyed music. My fellow townswoman, Josie Snow Barker, had a scrapbook of programs and invitations that gives proof of this. There is a program of a "Grand Musical Entertainment," with out-of-town talent, presented in 1879. (A Chickering concert grand pianoforte was hired for the two pianists.) In the first decade of the twentieth century, such groups as the Apollo Quartette, the Lotus Quartette, and the Boston Ideal Club presented programs in Blue Hill. Likely the first programs given by musical summer residents were those of 1895 and 1897. Dr. Junius Hill was the pianist and Mrs. Ward Peters was the soloist. Mrs. Peters's husband was Blue Hill–born, and a Boston lawyer. Sometimes a reader was brought in to add variety to the program. Holman Day, Maine novelist and poet, came at least once to Blue Hill.

Some of the concerts were given entirely by home talent. In 1896, the seniors of Blue Hill Academy presented a "Grand Entertainment." The proceeds were to help pay the expenses of graduation. A ticket cost fifteen cents. Often a concert by the natives was followed by a dance in which betasseled programs were used. Josie Barker's scrapbook holds such programs. They show that Josie was a belle of the 1890s. Her programs give the initials of her many admirers.

In the early nineteen hundreds, there were more musicians living at Parker Point than there were non-musicians. Mr. Nevin wrote of the Parker Point families: "The unique character of this settlement lies in the fact that it has become a stronghold for musicians of national renown. They are present in numbers and they love the place. They rest; they absorb the beauties and the pleasures of their surroundings; they gain needed strength for the season ahead." He went on to describe the arrival of the musical group, supposedly in chronological order. But he did not use a single date! "Many years ago" and "quite recently" are the expressions that he used to describe time.

I have made a list of musicians who I believe were in Blue Hill by 1908. There is no question that Professor Junius W. Hill of Boston, professor of music at Wellesley College, was the first musician to have a home on Parker Point. His cottage was probably the fourth or fifth one built there.

Wolf Fries was in Blue Hill by the summer of 1899. He had come to the United States in 1847 and came to Blue Hill because he was in poor health. A summer of walking and gardening cured his ills. The next year he returned and built a cottage. Every Sunday in the summer months, he sat in the choir loft of the Congregational Church and made sweet music on his cello. Blue Hill Congregationalists were displeased when a visitor from New York called the beloved cellist, "that old farmer sawing away in the back loft." Fries played in the Boston Symphony Orchestra.

Both Mr. and Mrs. Thomas Tapper had musical careers. He was a lecturer and a writer of musical textbooks. They were lovers of forest land and in time owned a hundred acres of land that extended back from the shore for half a mile.

Franz Kneisel had been summering in Vermont, but when he came to Blue Hill for his health, he decided that he liked Maine better. He built a cottage and was soon the largest owner of shore property among the summer people. He became a Blue Hill enthusiast and declared, "A violin string will last several times longer here than anywhere else." Members of his quartet followed him to Blue Hill. Kneisel influenced Henry Krehbiel, Dr. Horatio Parker, and Louis Bostelman to come to Blue Hill.

Krehbiel, a lecturer and writer, was for forty years the music critic for the *New York Tribune*. He was a gracious critic, always finding something nice to write about a performance. He had interests other than music. Nevin wrote of him; "Almost any day when he is not stewing on the golf links or on the deck of a sea-going fishing junk, or among his flowers, he can be found working in comfort at his musical work." When Krehbiel left on an early-morning fishing trip, Mrs. Krehbiel sang him off with lines from a Wagner opera.

Dr. Horatio Parker of Yale came to Blue Hill to recover from an attack of typhoid fever. His friends said that he quickly recovered but then had a severe attack of buying and building fever. Dr. Parker was a composer of oratorios and church music.

Maz Zack of the Boston Symphony Orchestra and Olive Mead, leader of the Mead Quartette, rented homes on Parker Point. The brothers Frank Damrosch, music educator, and Walter Damrosch, conductor, came often to visit the Kneisels.

Courtesy of Robert Sweetall

Kneisel's students followed their teacher to Blue Hill. Before 1908 some of the students stayed at the Blue Hill Inn. Among Kneisel's first students were Joseph and Lillian Fuchs, Sascha Jacobsen, and Florence Bryant. Some students boarded at John Snow's or the Pendleton House. But as the decades passed, more and more students rented village bedrooms and practiced in village parlors or in the woods. Twenty or thirty years later, some of them including Fritz Kreisler and Louis Levy became notable musicians.

I hope that little Julius Theodorowicz grew to be a successful musician. In one of Josie Barker's scrapbooks is a sheet of embossed paper on which these lines are written in beautiful script:

Presented to Julius Theodorowicz

for two hours practice upon his violin on Thursday 17th, 1905. May he always carry it in his pocket to remind him not to let any demoralizing influence take from him the gift that God has given him, or rob him in the smallest degree of his manhood.

I like to think that little Julius was a boarder at John Snow's. Perhaps the boy was homesick and Josie Snow Barker mothered him. Julius must have been a Kneisel student.

Mr. Kneisel was born in 1865 in Bucharest and studied at the Bucharest Conservatory and later at the Vienna Conservatory. He was generally known as "a distinguished Austrian violinist." In 1885 Wilhelm Gericke, the conductor of the Boston Symphony, invited him to Boston as the concert master of that orchestra. At the same time he founded the Kneisel Quartet. In 1905 Frank Damrosch, the director of the Institute of Musical Art (now the Juilliard School) in New York, asked Kneisel to assume the chair of its Department of Strings, which he held until his death in 1926. Felix Kahn built a concert hall and several studios in Blue Hill for his great friend Kneisel in 1922.

At most of the Kneisel concerts, Mr. Krehbiel lectured about the music played. In August 1909, the members of the music colony had a little fun. Under the name of Blue Hill Symphany [sic], they presented a two-part program. The first part included classical music and some English songs by Horatio Parker. The second part of the program was thus introduced: "A bit of musical pleasantry which shall be called

Fantasia Domestica

Grandma's Wedding 1850
Sounds from Garden and House 1854
Second Wedding circa 1880
Grandma's Dream of Youth
How Grandma Danced in Austria When She Was a
    Maid
Finale
The Old Order Remaining, There Are Prognostications for 1910"

There were thirty-five in an orchestra led by a former Pops conductor. Mr. Krehbiel blew a toy horn and someone rang the sleigh bells.

The Parker Point musical colony was not the only one in Blue Hill. East Blue Hill had its own musicians and students. Gaston and Edward Dethier and Louis Bostelman were East Blue Hill's master musicians. Probably Gaston

Dethier was the first to come. He had left his native Belgium about 1892 after he had been educated at the conservatories at Liege and Brussels. At the St. Louis Exposition of 1903 he had played the great organ, said to be the largest one in North America. In the same year, his brother Edward, a violinist, came to the United States. Both gave concerts in the early years of this century, and taught at the New York Institute of Musical Art and, after 1920, at the Juilliard School.

Gaston Dethier came to Blue Hill in 1906, Edward in 1907, and Louis Bostelman in 1908. All three spent the first summer in Blue Hill Village, where they boarded at the John Snow house. All three soon moved to East Blue Hill where they bought or built homes at the York Shore where Jean Dethier, a third brother, visited.

The Dethiers and Bostelmans had interests other than music. Charles Dethier, Edward's son, recalls that the three brothers were interested in golf. He wrote, "The three of

Courtesy of Robert Sweetall

them could often be found at the Blue Hill Country Club, or any near-by course, nattily dressed in plus fours, always wearing neckties, and competing fiercely. When the results were not up to anticipation, the air would be blue with stifled or noisy oaths, always in French." Mr. Bostelman, however, was a powerful swimmer. East Blue Hill young people crowded the shore to watch the musical swimmer give a perfect performance of "the Australian Crawl." When Mr. Bostelman decided that he would like to bathe in warmed salt water, Archie Long cut for him a mammoth tub from native granite, moved the tub to the York Shore on the ice of winter, and set the tub within the reach of the tide. The rising tide filled the tub with the icy water of the Atlantic. The sun and the warm air, when they were present, heated the water so that Bostelman could take a leisurely bath in his granite tub. Mr. Bostelman gave violin lessons to Long's son, Jerry, in return for the granite tub.

The music students of the three masters lived in the homes of East Blue Hill families, practiced in local parlors, and twice a week trudged up Hyer's Hill and then down to the York Shore for their lessons. Both the teachers and their students were generous in giving concerts for the benefit of the church and the library. Sometimes the concerts included readings by Mrs. Josephine Preston Peabody, who summered in East Blue Hill.

Jerry Long recalls that Mr. Bostelman now and then came to Mrs. Cora Long's parlor and played in the early hours of the evening. Neighbors sat on the porch and lawn and listened to Bostelman's playing. When the violinist finished, there was no applause, only sighs of satisfaction and soft words of appreciation. Mr. Bostelman founded the Blue Hill Chorale Society that included both summer people and natives.

Blue Hill also had "great music" in the summer produced

by amateur musicians in East Blue Hill. Dr. and Mrs. Seth Milliken, with the help of neighbors and friends "from away," put on in 1924, 1925, and 1927, performances of operas by Gilbert and Sullivan.

The Dethier brothers were active in the production of light operas that were presented at the Milliken Yacht Club. They liked to recall that one show went on during a rainstorm in which the piano, placed on the float, was nearly swamped by dashing waves and a rising tide.

Theodore Nevin, the early enthusiast who wrote articles for the *Pittsburgh Dispatch*, was a member of the Blue Hill summer colony and lived near Kneisel and the Tappers. He was no musician, but he was a prophet when he wrote: "What Chautauqua is for education, what Northfield is for religion, Blue Hill will be for music."

20

Worst Foot—Best Foot

BLUE HILL SUMMER PEOPLE, city-born and city-bred, sometimes had a problem adjusting to country ways and environment.

Mr. E. J. Brooks, our Friend's Corner neighbor, had been in his bungalow only a week when he got himself in trouble. One afternoon, he went to his back porch and saw men in a boat fishing off his shore. He called to his son, "Win, bring me the bullhorn." Once he had the horn at his mouth, he shouted: "You men get away from my beach. I want no fishing off my property." The fishermen had no bullhorn. They needed none. They cupped their hands around their mouths and shouted back to Brooks. They made it clear that he owned neither the beach nor the adjacent waters. They made it clear that they considered him an undesirable addition to the town.

Mr. Brooks exchanged his bullhorn for his cane and walked as fast as his short legs and weight allowed to a native neighbor's house. He appealed to the man of the house, "What did I do wrong?" The native answered, "Everything." Then he explained to the rusticator the rights of fishermen. It was several years before Mr. Brooks lived down his confrontation with the mackerelers.

A first-year resident of Parker's Point brought her servants with her, but she employed a native to mow her lawn, tend her garden, and row her up to town for the mail. One morning, she called to him, "Pull in the boat. I want you to row me up town for the mail."

The man continued to pull weeds and he called back, "Can't go. The tide's out."

She replied: "Never mind the tide. When I tell you to row me up town, I expect you to obey."

Up jumped the man from his knees. He snapped to attention and with mocking deference said, "Yes, Ma-dám."

In a few minutes woman and man were in the rowboat. He plied the oars with expert strokes. She grasped her shade hat with determined grip. They faced the mountain and the village. To the right they saw the cemetery gray with granite and marble, and to the left the Dodge farmhouse with its green meadows sloping down to the sea. They saw the town wharf but they never reached it. The boat grounded .in the mud a hundred feet from the wharf.

Neither rower nor passenger said a word. He pulled out the oars and placed them on the bottom of the boat. She removed her shoes and set them side by side on the bottom of the boat and, with her mailbag under her arm, she straddled over the side of the boat to the flats. It was a muddy walk to the shore, but she made it. It was embarrassing to enter the post office with no shoes and with stockings besmirched with mud. The row back to the cottage was silent.

That trip for the mail changed the relationship between employer and employee. Thereafter, she gave fewer orders.

She made requests and they were usually modified by such clauses as "if you are not too busy" or "if you find it convenient" or "if the tide is right." He never again called her "Ma-dám." He called her "The Mrs." And he spoke with admiration.

Mr. Brooks had put his worst foot forward the first week of his residency. But for hundreds of following summer weeks, his best foot was evident. He encouraged his neighbors to use his road to the shore. He was quick to ask them for advice. Neighborhood children received fruit and candy and Nabisco wafers from his generous hand. When searchers spent hours looking for children lost in the woods, he invited the men, at the conclusion of their successful search, to come to the bungalow for food. He gave each man a ten-dollar bill. He said to a native neighbor, "I count on you to tell me when there is any family having a hard time because of fire or sickness. I'll give you some bills to help them out. No need to mention my name. Just tell them that one of your friends sent the money."

A native often put his worst foot forward. Some were quick to call a summer person a snob, quick to ridicule a summer person's unfamiliarity with country ways. He might be quick to point out a summer person's ignorance of tides and weather. Perhaps he would be slow to respond to a newcomer's friendliness. He was sometimes slow to express thanks for money given to the hospital or the church or the library.

The adjustment of summer person and native to each other came rapidly and happily when humor seasoned the relationship. Franz Kneisel, the violinist, was one of the best-liked of the early summer people. He enjoyed the natives and he cultivated friendships with many of them. He and John Snow, the village innkeeper, became close friends. It was not love of music that united them. It was love of a good story and trout fishing. Every week from mid-June to late September, the musician and the innkeeper trudged to Peters's Brook with fishing poles in their hands.

One year Rufus, Mrs. Kneisel's gardener, had a young man to assist him. One day as Mr. Kneisel was practicing, he noticed that the new workman was idle. After a time, the musician went to the window and the following conversation took place:

"What are you doing?"

"Helping Ruf."

"What is Ruf doing?"

"Northin'."

Another afternoon Mr. Kneisel noticed the new helper leisurely weeding a flowerbed under a window of the practice room. The window was open. It pleased the musician to have a listener. When he finished playing a difficult piece, he went to the window and asked the workman, "Well, how did you like that?"

The weeder slowly rose to his feet so that he and his employer were eye to eye. He gave a quick reply, "Pretty good, Mr. Kneisel. But I wish you could hear my uncle play 'The Turkey in the Straw.'"

Now, in the last years of the twentieth century, descendants of the early summer people still come to Blue Hill for the summer. Some now spend the winter in town. Some have married natives. Many live on property once owned by their grandparents and great-grandparents. It seems improper to call them "summer people." They are Blue Hillers.

21

A Child's View of the Summer People

I CANNOT REMEMBER WHEN I did not know the Brooks family and the Curtis family, the first summer people to live in the Friend's Corner neighborhood.

There was a link of relationship between the two families. The ladies had once been Miss Josephine and Miss Mary Mudge. Never were sisters less alike. Mrs. Brooks's interests centered on matters domestic, and she oversaw the preparation of every meal. No cold potato and no half-orange went unused in her household. She spent a part of each forenoon on the household accounts and her cook-books. In the afternoon, she sat on the porch and rocked. Mrs. Curtis's interests ran to books and she left kitchen affairs to her cook. She spent part of every morning reading German. In the afternoon, she swam or walked or played with her children. One afternoon a week, she entertained guests in the granite teahouse.

Mrs. Brooks entertained her siblings and they usually stayed all summer. There was Lila Mudge, an unmarried sister; Robert Mudge, a bachelor; and Gordon Mudge, a widower. I imitated my friend Jane Curtis and called them "Aunt Lil" and "Uncle Bob" and "Uncle Gordon." "Aunt Lil" picked berries for her exercise. The Mudge brothers walked and swung the silver-headed canes provided by their affluent brother-in-law.

Mr. Brooks and Mr. Curtis were as different as were their wives. Mr. Brooks was a manufacturer who had been raised in poverty. He liked to oversee his farmer and chauffeur and the men whom he hired by the day, but he never touched a shovel or a spade or hoe. Mr. Curtis's family had had some means and had sent him to Harvard. But he liked to do farm work. He laid a wall; he worked in the garden; he drove the oxen. Mr. Brooks had no interest in travel and languages, art, and music. Mr. Curtis was interested in all four. Mr. Brooks took a great interest in politics. In 1912 he left the Republican party and joined the Bull Moose party of Theodore Roosevelt. Politics bored Mr. Curtis.

My father and mother were devoted to Mr. and Mrs. Brooks. My father had sold the Friend property to them. Father and Mr. Brooks had a close relationship — in fact, so close that Father followed Mr. Brooks into the Progressive party. Mother admired Mrs. Brooks both as a woman and a housekeeper. Mrs. Brooks was very generous to my family. At Christmastime she sent us gifts. When she came in late June, she brought more gifts. When she left in September, she presented what she called "my going-away presents." Her presents to me were items of clothing, always lacy and embroidered and bright in color. Mr. Brooks was also generous. When he went home in the fall, he gave a generous check to both the Congregational and the Baptist Church. The Blue Hill correspondent to the *Ellsworth American* took pains to report the fact. Mr. Brooks liked to entertain on a large scale. When he doubled the size of his barn, he gave a barn-warming. The affair included the presentation of a play — written for the occasion by Mary Chase — and produced by Miss Elinor and her friends. After the play, food and drinks (non-alcoholic) were served until midnight.

Mr. Brooks's most popular entertaining was done on August Sundays when he held religious services at the bungalow. The dining area and the living room were really one large room with a huge chimney in the center. The open staircase had a landing midway between upstairs and downstairs. The landing was a suitable place for the preacher and pulpit. Folding chairs for the congregation were placed in the big room and on the porches where open windows allowed the sound of the preaching to penetrate.

One Sunday was "Mission Sunday." The *Sunbeam*, the Mission boat, brought the Rev. Angus McDonald, the preacher, and Mrs. Peaslee, the teacher for the Seacoast Mission Society, to Blue Hill. They dined at the Brooks bungalow. At four o'clock people came from far and near to the service. Even as a very small child, I loved to listen to Mr. McDonald preach. His sermons included stories of sick islanders brought to the mainland for treatment and tales of sailors saved from the sea. We always sang the hymn with the stirring line, "Oh, Master, hear us when we pray to thee for those in peril on the sea."

After the service, everyone went to the porch or lawn, where the maids passed cups filled with lemonade and Miss Elinor and her friends, clad in gowns of water ribbon and chiffon, passed around cookies sent from S. S. Pierce of Boston. At the final church service there was a special treat, Mrs. Thurlow's ice cream, ordered from Rockland.

I was also devoted to the Curtis family and in the years of my childhood, I spent hours and hours in their home. Jane was two years younger than I. If I did not go to the Curtis house uninvited, Jane and her nursemaid came up to summon me. It was a revelation to me to be in a family where there were four teenagers and three maids. I loved to listen to Mr. Curtis and Helen play classical music. I was entertained when young Gordon and Robert quarreled and I was pleasantly startled when Mr. Curtis shouted at his older children. Mr. Curtis was a dramatic person, given to doing the unexpected and unusual. His older children stood in some awe of him. But not little Jane. She and I played in his office, forbidden territory to the older children. She and I used his top hat and ivory-headed cane in our games.

When Jane grew too old to have a nursemaid, she, my cousin Olive, and I used to play together. One of our pastimes was to sit at the edge of the road outside the Curtis hedge and watch for the East Blue Hill summer people. Every day except Sunday they drove to the Head-of-the-Bay to shop. We came to know the morning shoppers by looks and by name.

We recognized the Penders. He was a professor at Yale. He and Mrs. Pender drove in an open car with their yellow hunting dog in the back seat. Professor and wife did not look at us children. Nor did the dog. We knew that the dog sometimes jumped from the car to bathe in the drinking trough at Mr. Brooks's spring, and that the professor and Mr. Brooks had had words over the dog's trespassing. We decided that Mr. Brooks was right. We decided that we did not like the Penders and when they drove by, we stuck out our tongues at them.

We liked Mr. Andrews, whom we called "Uncle Santa Claus" because of his long white beard. He rode in the back seat of a car driven by a liveried chauffeur. The top of the car was always up. We decided that the top was up in order to keep the wind from blowing Mr. Andrews's beard. We waved wildly at him and he waved wildly back.

We recognized Mrs. Milliken when she drove by. We felt that we knew her because we went to the parties she had for her little Alida. Her chauffeur drove the car and she sat in the back seat. A duster protected her gown and a flowing veil came from her hat. The car slowed down and she spoke a few words to us. When it speeded up, we waved demurely. We cared very much for Mrs. Milliken's good opinion.

We knew the Slaven car at once because it was the largest. If Madam Slaven was the passenger in the back seat, we bowed ceremoniously and she bowed. Herman Gray, the chauffeur, looked straight ahead. But if Miss Nila, the daughter, was the passenger, we swung our arms. Miss Nila smiled and waved. To our great delight, "Herm" raised his hat.

The two Dethier families of musicians lived at the York Shore. In native speech, their name underwent a sea change and became "Der Chair." We children did not know Mr. Gaston from Mr. Edward. We did not recognize Mrs. Edward. But we knew Mrs. Gaston. Our parents would have been horrified had they known that we called her "Marie." When she returned from doing her shopping, she often drove her car off the road, got out, and came to sit with us on the dusty grass. She was always hatless and wore bright cotton dresses. She was tall and her hands were long. She always gave us cookies or crackers. Sometimes she helped us make a daisy chain or arrange a bouquet of wildflowers. We were sorry when she left us. Sometimes we ran after her car and shouted fond farewells. Our mothers often said: "I don't understand how you manage to get so much dust in your clothing."

My childhood was richer because I knew the Brookses and the Curtises and caught fleeting glimpses of the village-bound shoppers. I saw the early summer people as gracious and generous, always interesting, and sometimes dramatic.

First Settlers and Sons

BLUEHILL, MAINE.

Courtesy of Robert Sweetall

22

The Name-Givers

THE HILL BEHIND THE HEAD-OF-THE-BAY was called blue and the bay in front of it was named for the hill long before the first settlers came. When sailors came in from the deep sea, Mount Desert Rock was their first sighting of land. Having reached the Rock, they looked toward the blue hill, some thirty miles distant. The hill was the landmark that they followed to harbor and to home. Farmers in sight of the blue hill also looked at it. A clear top meant a good day for planting or haying. A fog-covered top meant rain. The hill was the weather marker that they watched from season to season. The hill became more and more important to them. Soon they were calling it Blue Hill Mountain.

The town's first name-giver was the legislature of the colony of Massachusetts. In 1762, the legislature designated it as Number 5 of the twelve David Marsh Townships laid out between the St. Croix and the Penobscot Rivers and granted to veterans of the war with France. The settlers preferred to call their township New Andover, then Newport. By 1777, the name Blue Hill Bay displaced Newport.

When the town was incorporated in 1789, it took the name of Bluehill. For the next forty-nine years, would-be name-changers tried to change the name. Once they went so far as to present a petition to the Maine legislature. The agitation for change was very strong in the 1830s when Nathan Ellis, Bushrod Hinckley, and Moses Clough led a drive to have the town called Hanover. Other names suggested from time to time were Fairport, Maine, Florence, and Lockport.

Jonathan Fisher's journals show that by 1800 certain names were associated with various areas of the town: the Neck (South Blue Hill); the Falls, at one time called the Fire Falls; Parker's Point; Head-of-the Bay (the location of the present village); Back of the Mountain (North Blue Hill); the Eastward (area to the east of the mountain); and McHard's (East Blue Hill).

By 1835, the year that Fisher stopped keeping a journal, names of the early settlers had become names on the land: Darling's Island, Jed's Island, Woods Point, Peters Cove, Peters Corner, Peters's Point, Peters Brooks (Big and Little), Carleton's Cove, Carleton's Hill, Marshall Hinckley's Hill, Tenney's Hill, Bragdon Brook, McHard's Stream, Hyer's Hill, Mason's Hill, Closson Point (also called Point Zenas), Clough's Hill, Conary Cove, Morse Hill, York Shore, Webber's Cove, and Oakes Brook.

A section of the town came to be called Grindleville. The Greene family moved from Surry, bought the Treworgy house atop a steep hill, and gave their name to the hill. A Scotch family, drawn here by the granite work, gave the name of Leith to a hill midway between the Head-of-the-Bay and McHard's.

The large ponds in town were marked First, Second, Third, and Fourth. With the passage of time, First Pond became Billings; Second Pond became Douglass; Third became Wood's. The Gray family settled near Fourth Pond. It is regrettable that the pond did not become Gray's Pond.

Three other ponds have interesting names. One of them is the Chalk Pond. Jonathan Fisher wrote about it: "In the N. E. part of the town is a pond, at the end of which, from the bed of a small brook, four or five feet deep, is taken a species of earth, resembling, when wet, a bluish-white paste; this rolled into a ball and dried or burned in the fire, becomes excellent chalk, especially for carpenters' use, having no sensible grit to wear out the line. It is also valuable for scouring silver, black-tin and the like." Fisher and his boys often went to the pond for the mud. The Chalk Pond has been called both Norris Pond and Noyce Pond.

Fisher wrote of the Salt Pond: "Blue Hill Bay communicates with a long salt pond, extending way back into Nas-

Courtesy of Robert Sweetall

keag Plantation, now Sedgwick." The outlet of the Salt Pond is over falls where the power was once used to turn both the wheels of a sawmill and a gristmill. Not far from the Salt Pond is a little pond with the name of Motherbush Pond. It is drained by a brook of the same name that flows into the Salt Pond.

Every town of the nineteenth century had a Mill Brook. According to Fisher, there were four brooks in town where there were mills in the early years of the nineteenth century. The brook at the Head-of-the-Bay had the power for five mills and so deservedly was called "the Mill Brook." McHard's Stream, Great Peters's Brook, and Carleton's Stream all had one or two mills. In later years there was a mill on that portion of Carleton's Brook between Douglass and Billings Ponds.

As the years went by, neighborhoods came to bear family names. In North Blue Hill there were four neighborhoods: the Wescott, the Hinckley, the Witham, and the Billings. Each had its own school that bore the name of the neighborhood. The neighborhood between East Blue Hill and Surry was the Webber neighborhood. That near East Blue Hill to the west was called the Friend's Corner neighborhood.

Meadows Brook and the Heath Brook, both flowing into McHard's Brook, are lovely names. In my childhood *heath* was given the old English pronunciation of "haith," thus making the name even lovelier. Motherbush is a good-sounding name and it arouses one's imagination. Popular tradition enlivens two names. There is a small island in Wood's Pond that is called Phoebe Anne Island. The story goes that Phoebe Anne was in a dory that was overturned and she drowned. There is the suspicion that poor Phoebe was murdered. There are two stories about the origin of the name the Kingdom. One story allows that the neighborhood was so called because Andrew Wood owned so much land. I prefer the second story: Andrew Wood was a giant of a man and he was as gentle as a kitten. He never raised his voice in anger or his hand in violence. One year a man moved into the neighborhood. The newcomer was vulgar, profane, and abusive. The neighbors said to Andrew, "You lick him. He deserves a licking. You could give him one. Go ahead and lick him and we'll crown you king of the neighborhood." The years passed and Andrew did not raise his hand against the rough character. Then one day his patience snapped. He gave the man a licking. His neighbors crowned Andrew king of the neighborhood. His neighborhood came to be called the Kingdom.

There is an interesting story, a true one, about Mrs. Hyer who gave her name to the steep hill beside McHard's Cove. She came from Canada and arrived in the deep of winter. She was walking and carrying on her back a small baby bundled in shawls. The child was probably not hers. She was not without money. She had a small house built for herself and child at the top of the steep hill. She brought up the baby, whom she called John Miller. Grown to manhood, he went to sea, in time owned his own schooner, and built a house for himself and family at the foot of Hyer's Hill.

The grandsons and great-grandsons of the first settlers were often shipbuilders and ship owners. They no doubt built beautiful and seaworthy vessels. But they chose uninteresting names for their vessels, usually the names of the owners: *Reuben Dodge, Andrew Witham, Jedidiah Holt, Jonah Holt, Jeremiah Holt, George Stevens, Doctor Fulton, Giles Wood, Lemuel Perers, Francis Cousins,* and *E. K. Chase.* The names of a few of the vessels show some imagination: *Zodiac, Unicorn, Equator, Trade Wind,* and *Albatross.*

Blue Hillers were traditional name-givers when it came

to choosing place names and ship's names. In the matter of naming their sons and daughters they showed originality. Of course they used Bible names and they often shortened them. Obediah became Obed; Ebeneazer became Eben; Jonathan became John. Phoebe and Hannah were popular names. But parental name-givers sometimes showed a fondness for very unusual names: Chesley, Cenova, Azor, Clarinda, Cheever, Nabby, Adelphi, Melinda, Roxana, Ingerson, Sylvanus, Archsah, Asero, Ashman, Edsley, and Marble.

Some families had a name-giving peculiarity. The Holts showed great fondness for the letter "J" when they named their male children Jonah, Jeremiah, and Jedediah. It was not uncommon to give a son more than one middle name. There was Reuben George Washington Dodge and Rufus George Frederick Candage and Thomas Jefferson Napoleon Holt. It was a common practice to name a child for well-known town figures such as Jonathan Fisher, George Stevens, and John Peters. Some families showed a grim determination to use a certain name. If little Dolly or little Isaac died in babyhood, the next baby girl was named Dolly; the next baby boy was named Isaac.

Great ships are no longer launched and named in Blue Hill. First names popular in the late eighteenth century and the nineteenth century have long been out of use. But the names that the first settlers gave the neighborhoods, hills, ponds, and brooks are still on the land.

23

The Darlings, A Founding Family

THE FIRST MEN to settle at the head of Blue Hill Bay, in 1762, were squatters. They were Joseph Wood and John Roundy and they occupied land to which they had no legal right, either by grant or by purchase. A statement by the Massachusetts Assembly has this sentence: "Captain Joseph Wood and sons and John Roundy came and settled at Bluehill bay before the land was either granted or Layed out." In a few years Wood bought land and the rights of a proprietor. Roundy bought land only. The proprietors were expected to set up a Congregational Church and establish a school. They had the right to set up local government and deed undivided lands to themselves or others.

No new settlers joined Wood and Roundy in 1762, but in 1764 Nathan and Marble Parker came. By 1770 there were thirty-one families and elder sons living in Township Number Five. The family names were those that were to be familiar for a century or more: Johnson, Clay, Hinckley, Horton, Candage, Osgood, Peters, Parker, Holt, Fisher, Dodge, Friend, Carleton, Roundy, Wood, and Darling.

The Darling family is one of the most interesting of the pre-1770 families. The Darlings were nonconformists and dared to do the unexpected. They were versatile and would try their hand at anything. They usually married women "from away" and often left town to seek their fortune. They were the first to ship granite from town and the first to recognize and advertise Blue Hill's mining resources.

Jonathan Darling, the first of his family to live in Number Five, was the son of a man who had fought with Pepperrell at the siege of Louisburg in 1746 and died there. The great fort was captured from France but returned at the end of that war. It is not surprising that Jonathan Darling took part in the later siege of Louisburg. The second Darling kept a record of the twenty months he stayed on Cape Breton Island, laying siege to the fort and guarding it after the colonial victory. In 1760 he returned to the home of an uncle in Massachusetts. By 1762 he was looking for a place to settle and he spent the summer and fall of that year in Maine exploring the region of the Great and Little Ossipee rivers. He returned to Andover, and in the winter of 1763 he courted the daughter of Nicholas Holt. In September he married Sally Holt and wrote in his diary, "I removed to my father Holt's house for the winter." (Holt was a man of property and education who also moved to Number Five and became the leader of the first generation of settlers.)

In 1762 the Massachusetts General Court granted twelve townships in eastern Maine to the veterans of the wars with the French. These coastal townships stretched from the Penobscot River to the St. Croix. It appears that Jonathan Darling was not one of the original grantees. It is probable that he bought his land from a grantee who chose not leave his Andover or Braintree home.

Jonathan Darling made a brief record of his move to Number Five:

April 12—Set sail for East Andover.
April 15—Reached East Andover.
May 21—Began to clear for a farm.
May 27—Wife arrived with my effects. [She came with her father, Nicholas Holt.]
July 29—My house raised.
Sept.19—Moved into my house.

Jonathan Darling was the first man to clear land on the east side of the bay below the Narrows. John Peters was his neighbor on one side; Seth Kimball was his neighbor on the other side. Jonathan's house faced the bay and had a view of Long Island. Whales played off his shore and an Indian shell heap was on his beach.

Jonathan Darling was a man of energy. The valuation of Blue Hill in 1790 shows that he was a man of property:

20 Acres Mowing	2 2Year Olds
15 do. Pasturing	5 yearlings
540 do Wild Land	2 Hogs
2 Oxen	1 House
10 Cows	1 Barn

The total valuation of his property was 147 pounds and 12 shillings.

Jonathan Darling was also a man of some education. In the Massachusetts archives there is a letter that he wrote to a Mr. Stevens, a non-resident grantee who complained that the resident committee that had laid out Number 5 "shuffled into their own hands and and into the hands of a few particular friends between 1500 and 2000 acres of the best land of the Township." Mr. Darling gave specific directions on how Stevens should proceed to let his grievances be known to the Massachusetts government. Darling himself was not well pleased with the division of land. He wrote Stevens, "They would pick me a lot that is nothing but a mountain of rocks not worth a sixpence." Darling was wrong, dead wrong. His son and his grandson and others were to quarry thousands of dollars worth of granite from the "mountain of rocks."

Jonathan Darling and Sally had eight children who inherited a tendency to leave the place of their birth. Jonathan Junior moved to Enfield in 1820 and his sister Mary soon joined him. Samuel went to Enfield but left behind his son Anson for his father to bring up. Jedediah became a preacher and went to Ellsworth to live, but in a few years he returned home, gave up preaching, and became a businessman. Grandson Anson followed the sea and prospered. He built a large house in a meadow on his grandfather's land. He and one of his sons were lost on the brig *Randolph* when it went down in the Bay of Biscay. Jedediah, the one-time preacher, had a son who moved to Franklin. A second son, Vespasian, went to Portland where he became the circulation manager of the city's largest newspaper. Three of Jedediah's sons stayed in Blue Hill. Jedediah Junior outdid all the other Darlings in originality, versatility, and energy. He legally changed his name to Byron Whitefield Darling. He was a schoolteacher, music master, state legislator, and colonel of the First Regiment of the First Brigade of the State Militia. When Blue Hillers marched off to fight in the so-called Aroostook War, he accompanied them as far as

Bangor. He served as a county coroner, deputy sheriff, and deputy collector of customs. In a town that in his lifetime was first Whig and then fiercely Republican, he was a Democrat. But at the time of the Civil War he was a "War Democrat" and a strong supporter of the Union. When Lincoln was assassinated, the entire front of the Darling house was decked in black. With his father and brothers, he was in the granite business. He became interested in mining and in his old age he collected early records and wrote historical articles. Byron's brothers William and Frederick stayed in Blue Hill and, like Byron, lived in the village.

As early as 1816, Jedediah Senior had started quarrying granite in East Blue Hill, not far from the cove. The granite taken from this quarry, called "the Eagle Quarry," was sent to Boston. A few years later he and his sons had three quarries nearer the village. One quarry, called the "Door-stone," was above the road. The other two were on the shore. The father built a large granite house for his family. The Darling Blue Hill Granite Company got out granite for buildings in Ellsworth, Pittsburgh, Washington, D.C., Eastport, and New York City. The paving ordered by the city of New Orleans was delivered but never paid for. After the Civil War the Darlings reorganized under the name of J. Darling and Sons. Their best customer was Joseph Westcott and Son, a Blue Hill granite company that had moved to Portland.

By 1876, William H. Darling and Frederick A. Darling, who had earlier been involved in quarrying granite, began to buy up land between Second (Douglass) and Third (Wood's) Pond. They probably prospected for minerals. They did not need to fan popular interest in mining; others were doing that. In 1876, the *Ellsworth American* labeled Blue Hill as "the most metalliferous town of Hancock

County." In 1879, William Stewart, a Nevada miner turned lecturer, dazzled Hancock County with his oratory. He said of Blue Hill, "There is possibly no spot on the planet where mining can more expeditiously be carried out."

So was born Blue Hill's mining boom. By 1880 there were thirty mining companies more or less active in town. The village had a building boom. An old boardinghouse was given a third story and was called the Copper and Gold Exchange. New stables, stores, and houses were built. William Darling promised people that he would build a bank and a hotel and bring electricity to town. William Darling wore a diamond ring, drove fast horses, moved into a larger house, and took pride in being the director of twelve Blue Hill mines and of one mine in New Hampshire.

The copper mines were two miles west of the village. Near the mines, shacks were built for married men and their families. More prosperous men, like the four Astbury brothers, Thomas, Robert, William, and Samuel, from Canada, built comfortable farmhouses. A boardinghouse, mills, tramways, and engine houses were built. Blue Hill mines became a mecca for the curious. Excursion parties came by steamboat to Blue Hill and then hired buckboards to take them to the mines. Others came by train or stage to Ellsworth and there hired horse-drawn vehicles to take them to Blue Hill.

The Douglass mine was the most prosperous. But by 1888 the boom was over. Overexpansion, overspeculation, hard times, and in some cases bad management caused the collapse of the mining boom. Writing in the *New England Quarterly*, Virginia Chase Perkins expressed it this way: "Slowly, mining towns returned to normal. There was no smoke to darken them, and no spans of horses disturbed the dust of the village streets. Most of the people wanted to forget the past."

But William Darling could not forget the past. He lamented and grieved and he still dreamed. When he became insane, his nephews took him to the insane asylum and sold his diamond ring and fast horses to support his wife.

In 1989 there are few people in Blue Hill who are descendants of Jonathan Darling. I am glad that two islands, Jed's and Darling's, memorialize this venturesome founding family.

The Copper and Gold Exchange.   *Courtesy of J. M. Hinckley*

24

Jonathan Fisher, Neighbor and Farmer

JONATHAN FISHER'S CONTEMPORARIES knew him as a preacher. Perhaps they feared him. They knew him as a craftsman, and they hired him to put names on their brigs and schooners. They bought from him tables, chairs, bureaus, and chests. They also knew him as a surveyor. He surveyed private property lines and laid out roads. His friends and neighbors knew him as a linguist and now and then heard him quote Greek, Latin, Hebrew, and French in his pulpit. They knew that he had invented a kind of shorthand for himself and perhaps wondered what good it was to him. They knew that he painted pictures. Perhaps they wondered how he found time for such "trifles." Certainly Fisher's contemporaries marveled at his talents, energy, and versatility.

And Fisher's contemporaries knew him as a neighbor, farmer, and father. Fisher's journals, from 1791 to 1835, give the details of the parson's life in his neighborhood, garden, and home. He wrote his journals in his shorthand. Gaylord Hall, a descendant, deciphered a few. Edith Weren deciphered more. More recently, William Hinckley deciphered others. The journals, not complete, are owned by the Fisher Memorial of Blue Hill, the Farnsworth Museum of Rockland, and others. They have not been published. Typewritten copies are owned by the Fisher Memorial and the Blue Hill Public Library.

Young Fisher, Massachusetts-born and Harvard-educated, spent the summers of 1794 and 1795 in Blue Hill, where he served as a temporary minister. The first summer, he lived at the home of Phineas Osgood, who lived near the foot of the mountain. Both summers he preached twice a week, called, and did surveying. In October 1795, he agreed to become the permanent minister. He left Blue Hill on October 29 and arrived in Boston on November 3. December was a whirlwind month for Fisher. He visited friends and relatives in various towns. He became engaged to Dolly Battle. As he expressed it: "The question of our future connection was settled." In February, he took Dolly to see his mother, Katherine Avery Fisher. After a winter of courting, visiting, and painting pictures, he returned to Blue Hill in May, having borrowed forty dollars from a Mr. Kirkland of Cambridge.

The summer of 1796 was one of the busiest of Fisher's life. He stayed in the home of Colonel Nathan Parker, where he had resided the previous summer. On July 13, he was ordained in Daniel Osgood's field on the Mill Brook. By August 26, five acres of his land were burned and ready for clearing. In September, the house was raised and a well, thirty-three feet deep, was completed. He preached twice a week, called on parishioners, visited Buckstown, went to

Castine to preach, and often worked on the unfinished church. On October 4th, he set sail for Boston. The journey was slow because of a bad storm and a stop in Portland. The brig did not drop sails in Boston until October 18th. The wedding was on November second and Parson Fisher, his bride, and Dolly Newell, Mrs. Fisher's little niece, left for Blue Hill on December second.

The Fishers spent their first winter in Blue Hill in Colonel Parker's house on the hill near the church. It was also near the ministerial lot. During his stay there, the parson worked on his house and the church, surveyed the Little Bay, walked to Newbury Neck to marry a couple, made a chest-chair for Dolly, preached twice a week, went to Deer Isle and Sedgwick, got out bark to sell to a tannery, walked to the Union River, and struck off bookplates for the books in the church library. On May 15th, the Fisher family was enlarged by the arrival of Seth Hewins, the parson's brother-in-law, who came to work for the Fishers at wages of two dollars a month. Hewins's first task was to take down the chimney in the Fisher house. It had proved to be of faulty construction. On November second of 1797, the Fishers moved into their home. Colonel Parker, ever the good neighbor, loaned his horse to move the Fisher belongings.

When Dolly and Jonathan moved into their home, their nearest neighbors were Joseph Wood (Junior), Robert Wood, Obed Johnson, Jedediah Holt, Nathan Parker, and Joshua Horton. Horton's name is the one that appears most often in the journals. The parson and Horton exchanged work. Fisher repaired Horton's tools. Horton loaned Fisher his horse. Mrs. Fisher went to Horton's to help Mrs. Horton make a dress. When the Hortons "went to the other side" and left Fisher's church, the parson grieved; Horton returned to the Congregational church. Horton's second break from Fisher's church was final. Baptist he became; Baptist he remained.

On the road to Penobscot, some two miles from Fisher's place, there lived three Hinckley brothers, Isaiah, Ebeneazer, and Nehemiah. In time, Isaiah and Ebeneazer became Baptists. But not the faithful Nehemiah. When Fisher called on recalcitrant church members, he often took along Nehemiah. When he drove to Penobscot, he always borrowed a Hinckley horse for the journey. He seemed to time his return to the supper hour. "Took tea at Nehemiah Hinckley's" is a frequent entry in Fisher's journal. When all the children, save little Polly and Dolly, were grown, Mrs. Fisher often went with her husband to Penobscot while their little girls were left with the Hinckleys.

In the late 1790s and early 1800s more settlers came to town and the Fishers had more neighbors at the Head-of-the-Bay. George and Theodore Stevens came. Both became members of Fisher's church and Theodore became a life-

1047 „The Parson Fisher House" Built 1796. Bluehill, Maine

Courtesy of Robert Sweetall

long deacon. The prosperous George soon became a Baptist, but he and Fisher continued to be friends. George provided a horse for the parson to ride or drive. George's workmen sharpened Fisher's tools and did his iron work. Fisher made two mill wheels for Stevens, surveyed the Stevenses' woodland, and often did errands for him in Buckston or Bangor. When Fisher was due to return from a trip on which he had used a Stevens horse, Mrs. Fisher walked to the Stevens home and waited for the return of her husband. When he got back, he and Dolly were always asked "to take tea" with George and his Dorcas.

About 1810, Nathan Ellis came to the Head-of-the-Bay and set up a store in the heart of the village. Fisher often went to the Ellis store. In 1818, Ellis married Dolly Newell, the niece of Mrs. Fisher. Dolly named her second son Jonathan.

Another new neighbor was Dr. Tenney, who by 1815 had moved from Sedgwick and occupied a house on the hill where stood Fisher's church. The Fishers had close relations with the doctor because they were often sick, but they also had friendly relations. Fisher often wrote in his journal during the 1820s: "Tenney children spent the evening with my children" or "The three little Tenney girls came to spend the night with my little girls."

Seth and Katherine Hewins bought land of the Fishers. While they built a house a little to the west of the Fisher house, they lived with the Fishers. Fisher was devoted to Seth and always spoke of him as "Brother Hewins." One can tell from the journal that Fisher and his sister Katherine were often at odds. Fisher mourned when the Hewins children died (likely from consumption). Perhaps the Hewins were too neighborly. In a letter written on May 13, 1837, Fisher wrote of the Hewins, "The family is very neighborly, calling in for something almost three hundred sixty five times in the year."

Fisher's neighbors exchanged work with him and loaned him a horse or a yoke of oxen. He wrote deeds, wills, and letters for them. In one instance, he wrote a confession for a woman—a confession of adultery. The church's action against the woman and her later denial of the adultery caused Fisher trouble. When the neighbors came to call, Mrs. Fisher sometimes brought in apples or pears or cherries for a special treat. Sometimes the parson cut with his own hand a melon for his guests.

Fisher in his journals and his neighbors used words that their forebears had brought from old England: a jag of hay, twitches of wood, fogged in, tarried, latter harvest, a spit of snow, kept my bed (stayed in bed), ruin (alders and thistles), near his end (near death), pissamire (an ant), fixing up (getting ready for a journey), posset (mixture of wine and curdled milk given the sick), garden sauce (fresh vegetables).

Fisher and his neighbors used local geographical terms. When they went to Portland or Boston, they spoke of "going westward." When they went to Ellsworth, they spoke of "going eastward." They called inner Blue Hill Bay "the Little Bay." The river in Ellsworth they called the "East River." Their "Castine River" was perhaps the Bagaduce. In his journal Fisher often wrote of the "Southern Bay."

The neighbors who gathered in the Fisher kitchen for an evening call would certainly have talked about the weather. Thanks to Fisher's journal, we know what they might have been commenting upon some months. It is probable that he did not own a thermometer; he never gave the exact temperature. "Very cold" and "blustery" were his expressions for chill weather. It is remarkable that in over thirty years of recording weather he never once wrote of summer heat, though once he did note the drought. I am inclined to believe that the parson liked hot weather because the heat meant good growing weather for his corn, rye, and wheat, grains that were ground to make flour for the family. Once he wrote to complain of a wet spell in August that caused his rye to rust. Frequently he noted thundershowers that wet the hay in the field.

Fisher and his neighbors talked about the February thundershower of 1803, the dreadful snowstorm (worst of the year) that came on April 16, 1805, and the great "blow" of October 3, 1805, that did five hundred dollars' damage in the town. "Eighteen-hundred-froze-to-death," the season of 1814–15, would have been much talked about because there was a frost every month of the year. On April 24 the ground froze hard and, as late as June 24, people wore mittens. Cattle starved the next winter because of the poor hay crop. Fisher and his neighbors would have talked about the earthquake of 1817, the October gale of 1826 that broke off the church chimney, and the freshet of April 1832, that carried away four mill dams in town.

Fisher's journal shows that he was a watcher of the night sky. Likely he talked to his callers about comets, meteors, planets, and rings around the moon. He once wrote of a "smokey fall" and another time he wrote of a "blue-green sun." Only once did he record a rainbow. It seems strange that he never referred to fog. In one of his poems he plainly had fog in mind but he took care not to use the word:

> For the morning mists are fled,
> Damps with eastern winds are gone,
> Smiling from his watery bed
> Rises now the morning sun.

Fisher and his visitors would have taken pleasure in talking about the building and launching of ships and brigs. Mrs. Fisher might have spoken with pride that a Holt brig was named for the two older Fisher daughters. The dedication of Blue Hill Academy in 1803, John Peters's gift of a bell to the church, and the building of the Holt Block in the 1830s were certainly topics for talk. The two Castine hangings and the murder trial of an Ellsworth doctor must have been exciting topics.

For years they would have talked of the British occupation of Castine in 1814, and the battle of Hampden, the cannon sounds of which were heard in Blue Hill. They would have recalled with anger how Blue Hill men were forced to surrender their rifles and shot to the British. They were returned only when the owners signed a paper agreeing not to fight the British.

There were topics of conversation that the talkers would have avoided: the death of three of the Fisher children and the 1806 division in the Congregational Church.

Perhaps Fisher told them about his trips to Massachusetts and how he visited Professor Popkin and took tea with President Willard of Harvard, how he had preached in a Boston church, inspected a prison and a factory, seen a steam engine, visited the Botanical Gardens in Cambridge, and heard about the telegraph. Perhaps he told about the trips that he and Dolly took to sell from house to house copies of his *Scripture Animals*. Certainly he spoke of his missionary journeys in Hancock, Penobscot, and Washington counties. In 1820, he likely spoke of his joy in being free from debt for the first time in his life.

Fisher's journals make clear that Fisher had good neighbors, and that he and his family were good neighbors.

Fisher's pictures, both in oil and watercolor, give evidence of his love for living things. His *Latter Harvest* shows corn, pumpkins, squash, and apples, all raised in his garden or orchard. In 1814 he painted by candlelight the picture of a red cow, fat, contented, and with dreamy eyes. The mountains and the trees in the picture are totally unlike his usual mountains and trees. In a few of his Harvard College pictures, there are shadowy cows in the background. He always kept two or three cows and each was given a floral name. It is evident that he liked cows.

Fisher's *Black Horse at Bluehill* shows the mountain in the background with a fence, a yellow and green house, and the corner of a red building (perhaps the meeting house) in the foreground. The bobbed-tailed mare is pawing with her forefoot as though eager to run. Her neck is too long for her body and her head too small for the neck. I suspect that the artist did not like horses. As a young man, he had often been thrown from the saddle. As an older man, he was involved in several carriage accidents that seem to suggest that he was a poor driver. Once his horse ran away with him.

His small paintings in his four notebooks show how interested he was in birds and beasts. Some of them were painted from nature, others were copied from English or French paintings. Fisher's major witness to his love of nature is his *Scripture Animals,* a book that he envisioned in his college days. The book was published in 1834 by William Hyde of Portland. He bought 625 of the thousand printed and he sold them himself by going from town to town. The book is illustrated by 140 woodcuts arranged in alphabetical order. Each cut is accompanied by a description and Bible verse. Now and then the parson included a bit of verse containing good advice. The woodcut of the cock has this verse:

When shrill clarion bids you rise,
Wake up your mental powers.
For meditation learn to prize
The cheerful morning hours.

Fisher, the nature lover, was an enthusiastic farmer. He spent hours in his workshop making tools and containers to use in his farm work. This is only a partial list: chains, pump, yoke, wheels, pig's trough, wall machine, sled runners, cask, drills, fitting for grindstone, shingle mill, shingle jack, scales, ladders, winnowing machine, axe handles, bark baskets, wheelbarrow, windmill, axle tree, harnesses, cider mill, sleds, and pulleys for a cheese press.

He never did his farm work alone. He always had men or boys to help him. In the early years, Seth Hewins was his helper. Fisher's three sons in turn helped him. Boys whom he boarded were supposed to help him. He often exchanged work with his neighbors. In his last years, Willard, his youngest son, took over the farming and surveying jobs. In 1834, Willard married Mary Norton, the oldest of Captain Norton's twenty-one children. The young Fishers lived in the parsonage and there was a division of the rooms. Likely the elder Fishers kept the study, the parlor, and the master bedroom.

It is probable that Fisher used steers for work in the field. Not until 1821 did he purchase a horse. It was plainly a driving horse. According to notations in the journal, the horse was more often used by Willard and his sisters than by the parson. The chaise was bought in 1820 with money that Mrs. Fisher inherited. Fisher took pride in building a chaise-house for the vehicle.

Fisher did not slaughter his farm animals. A neighbor was hired to do the grisly task. However, he did kill cats, often three or four at a time. The cat skins were cured and used on the place or sold. The ashes from the fires were used on the land or sold to Spofford's potash works on the town landing. Nothing was wasted at the parsonage.

The family at the parsonage was well fed. In later years, there were apples, pears, cherries, peaches, and plums from the orchard. There were vegetables from the garden, rye and wheat from the field. Corn, wheat, and rye were ground at the town mill for flour. Not until 1826 is there a record in the journal of the purchase of flour at the store. In the winter, the family had pork, veal, beef, and lamb, all frozen. There were bacon and salt pork. In the summer, there were trout, caught by Fisher. "Took my son Jonathan fishing" is a common entry in the journal. Later Josiah and Willard had their turns at fishing with their father. Fisher usually recorded the number of trout caught. Often he caught ten or twelve or fourteen. On July second, 1800, he caught a trout that weighed nine and a half pounds. Now and then, Mrs. Fisher bought fish from a peddler who came to the door. Fisher wrote in August 1824, "Mrs. Fisher bought a twenty-four pound halibut for thirty-nine cents." The Fisher boys shot pigeons and partridge for the family table. There were cranberries from the bog. By the 1830s, the bog produced so many berries that the surplus was sent to Boston to sell. It is plain that the Fishers were great drinkers of tea. In 1815, they purchased ten pounds of tea at one time.

It is surprising that neither hens nor eggs are mentioned in the journal. Perhaps keeping and tending the hens was Mrs. Fisher's work. One of Fisher's most endearing woodcuts is that of a hen, perhaps one in Mrs. Fisher's flock. Nor does Fisher ever write of digging or eating clams. He did not write of fishing for cunners and flounders in the home bay but he often fished when aboard a brig bound for Boston. He wrote of setting out maple trees and he commented upon their rapid growth. But he never wrote of tapping the trees for sap or boiling sap for the syrup.

When he was old, he wrote with delight: "Willard brought home a hive of bees today." So one may guess that Fisher himself was not a beekeeper. But he was a successful grower of melons. He wrote in his journals of the planting of the melon seeds and the growth of the plants. He rejoiced when the melons matured; every year, he counted the melons. Often in early October he wrote the sad comment, "Cut my last melon today."

Fisher and his boys often went afield to pick berries. Once they went to Long Island to pick blueberries. It is pleasant to think of their companionship as they walked, berried, and talked. Perhaps they rested in the shade and the father told his sons about picking berries in his childhood.

Fisher's journal reports nearly forty years of farming. The years did not pass without accidents due to wind and weather, animal depredation, and human carelessness. One year, rot spoiled the potatoes; another year rust blighted the rye. Frost often killed crops, especially in 1814–15. A night wind blew off the chaise-house door; careless driving caused the loss of a wagon wheel; a pail of ashes set the hog house afire. A bear killed some sheep; the cows broke out of the pasture and got into the garden; crops withered from lack of rain. Josiah twice dropped farm knives down the well. Willard once planted potatoes in hills where the day before his father had planted peas. Shade trees near the house caught fire; a thief stole sheep from the pasture; neighbors' hogs got out of their pen and invaded the Fisher garden.

Fisher's eyes were not blind to the wildflowers and seeds

of the field or to the bees and butterflies. He gathered pennyroyal and mullein that he dried and used for cough syrup and the making of poultices. In 1812, he picked two to three quarts of caraway seed. He gathered rose petals to make rose conserve. In 1813, he made thirteen ounces of the conserve.

The Fisher fields were first planted in 1797. Wildflowers were slow to appear. It was with evident pleasure that he wrote in 1817: "For the first time, after twenty years, flowers like an apron are in the field."

Perhaps Fisher was thinking of the bountiful harvest from garden and orchard, from field and berry patch, when he wrote: "Blessed be to God for prospering me on my way."

25

George Stevens,
Village Squire

GEORGE STEVENS AND JONATHAN FISHER were contemporaries. We know a great deal about Fisher. He kept a diary in which he recorded his chores, woes, and joys, the records of his journeys, and his views on such varied matters as raising melons and seeking salvation. Many of the letters that he wrote and received are available. He wrote poems, a sketch of his life, articles, and sermons. We know what books he read, and many of his books are in the Fisher house in Blue Hill.

Squire Stevens kept no diary and wrote no biographical sketch. The letters that he wrote have been destroyed. His library, if he had one, has long been scattered and destroyed. All that remains of what he wrote are his record books and a notebook of his childhood.

The Fisher journal shows that Fisher and Stevens saw each other often. Fisher often borrowed a horse from Stevens for his out of town trips. He often took his tools to Stevens's smithy for sharpening, and sometimes he borrowed tools from him. Once he asked Stevens to change a hundred-dollar bill for him. Now and then Fisher did errands for Stevens when he went to Buckstown or Bangor. The model of a shingle mill that Fisher made in 1824 was probably made for Stevens. When Fisher wrote in 1822 of taking seventy-five pounds of wool to the mill, the mill that he referred to was certainly the Stevens mill on Mill Brook.

George Stevens fathered no children, but he brought up one of his brother's sons. He also had a foster son who drowned when he was a student at Colby College. He and Jonah Holt suggested that the town have a music master to educate the children in "sacred music." They gave generously to a fund to pay for the master. George Stevens eventually left his "mansion house," mills, money, and wild lands (save that given to the Baptist Church) to found an academy. At the time that he made the will, the Blue Hill Academy was doing well. Perhaps the squire, a Baptist, resented the Congregational dominance of the board of trustees. Perhaps he had his doubts as to the financial stability of the school. Mrs. Mary Haskell Stevens, his second wife, had the use of his estate as long as she lived. Not until years after Stevens's death was his academy — merged with the old Blue Hill Academy — established. The building was designed by George Clough and built by George Butler at a cost of six thousand dollars. The record shows that George Stevens loved children.

Late in the eighteenth century George Stevens and his brother Theodore had come to the Head-of-the-Bay and built similar homes, both of which stand in 1989. Appropriately enough, Theodore's home is the Congregational parsonage. Theodore married Dorcas Osgood before he came to Blue Hill. George found another Dorcas Osgood after he came to Blue Hill. Theodore's Dorcas and George's Dorcas were cousins. Theodore was a blacksmith; George was a businessman with numerous irons in the fire. He gave land to Theodore's sons and he remembered them in his will. Likely he was pleased when two of his nephews built homes not far from his. The record shows that George Stevens was devoted to his brother and his brother's family.

George Stevens was a shipbuilder, his yard being on the west side of the village's harbor. One source states that he was his own master builder. In Parson Fisher's "Morning View of Bluehill" one can see the squire's yard with a ship on the ways. Stevens built and owned the *Magnolia* and other vessels, two of which bore his name. He built and was part owner of the *Orion, Jasper, Grandee, Maine, Eolian, Elizabeth,* and *Ocean Ranger.* He brought to town Thomas Lord as a workman in his shipyard. But Lord soon graduated from building ships to building houses and churches.

Courtesy of Robert Sweetall

Stevens was also a mill owner on Mill Brook. Before the War of 1812 he built a cotton factory that stood on the east side of the brook near a dam, the remains of which are still evident. This so-called Factory Dam held water as late as 1869. Cloth was not manufactured in the cotton factory. The factory ginned the cotton, spun threads, and wound together the warp which was sent to larger mills to make cloth or carpeting or canvas. When the War of 1812 broke out, Stevens had a great supply of warp on hand. The war forced up the price of cotton and Stevens made a handsome profit. He also owned a fulling mill that shrank, smoothed, and straightened homespun cloth.

Stevens was often in business with others. He and five others at one time owned a sawmill at the mouth of the Mill Stream. At one time, he and John Peters and Nathan Ellis owned most of Long Island. He encouraged others to go into business. He sold land on the Mill Stream to Ezra Curtis, a wheelwright; Matthew Ray, a blacksmith; and Robert Osgood, a cabinetmaker.

George Stevens lived in colorful times. He saw the decline of the Federalist party and the rise of the Democratic party. He was a Whig and an admirer of John Quincy Adams and Daniel Webster. He was angered by the British seizure of Castine in the War of 1812. He watched Blue Hill men march away to take part in the so-called Aroostook War with Canada, and he argued the issues of the annexation of Texas and the war with Mexico. Like most other New Englanders, he probably opposed both. I would doubt he was a strong critic of slavery. After all, he purchased cotton from the South. He saw Blue Hillers drawn to the gold mines of California and watched the growing ill will between the North and South over the extension of slavery in the territories. He died too soon to see steam drive sail from the sea or to know that the rocky acres of New England could not compete with the rich lands of the West.

We know less about George Stevens than we know about Jonathan Fisher, but this we do know about the squire: He loved children, his family, and his town. He was a successful businessman at a time when his country was burgeoning with change and opportunity.

26

Thomas Lord, Builder

THOMAS LORD, joiner, housewright, and architect, belonged to the second wave of settlers who came to Blue Hill. Unlike most of the first settlers, he did not come from Massachusetts — he came from Surry. Most likely he bought his village house lot from George Stevens. He cut no timber; he farmed no fields. He devoted the fifty-two years of his working life to building. Two months before he died in 1880, he summed up his life work thus: "Have worked on 83 vessels, more or less, built 84 dwelling houses, 12 school houses, 14 meeting houses, 15 barns and sheds, and other public buildings, 10 stern mouldings and heads and blinds and other works."

Lord left school when he was fifteen years old and went to Ellsworth where he drove a horse and ground bark in a tannery. Then he lived with an uncle on whose farm he worked and in whose vessel he sailed. Not until he was twenty-two years old did he become apprentice to a carpenter. It was George Stevens, Blue Hill's leading citizen, merchant, and shipbuilder, who brought him to Blue Hill to work in his shipyard.

Thomas Lord's papers and diary, now owned by his descendants and Colby College, show that he was a bad speller and a poor handwriter, but that he was nevertheless a careful record keeper and a man who took pride in his work.

Thomas Lord is best known as a builder of churches. The first church that he built was the Congregational Church in Blue Hill, constructed in 1841 after fire destroyed the first church, which was at the top of Tenney's Hill. Among Lord's papers are the plans for this church: drawings by Bangor architect Benjamin Deane and sketches from Edward Shaw's *Rural Architecture*, published in 1843. This church is a Greek Revival structure, correct in every respect. It is all the more beautiful because its decoration is sparse. The interior of the church was done over late in the nineteenth century by George Clough, a Blue Hill man who had become the architect for the city of Boston. Six stained-glass windows eventually displaced the many paned windows that Lord had put in place.

The Blue Hill Baptist Church across the village from the Congregational Church was not built by Lord, though local tradition credits it to Lord. The Baptist Church was built in 1816–17 when Thomas Lord was a child. Parson Fisher's *Morning View of Bluehill*, painted in 1824, shows the Baptist Church, a yellow structure with windows in the back and a belfry at the center of the roof. In the 1850s Lord removed the "table leg finish" in the interior and remodeled it. He did away with the windows on the back and removed the belfry. He did over the exterior and built a tower and steeple at the front. Only in a few respects did the changes conform to his work in the Congregational Church. The towers of the churches are similar. The pulpit and its surroundings in the Baptist Church resemble those in Lord's first church, but they are heavier and more ornate.

Thomas Lord was a member of the Baptist Church. His original employer, George Stevens, was the church's most generous supporter. By remodeling it, Lord perhaps wished to show his love and enthusiasm for his church. He incorporated his own ideas and plans and made no attempt at architectural conformity. For the first time he used a carved rosette with flanking curves as an ornament. This motif came to be Lord's trademark and signature. He used it in his own home, in the churches in Brooklin and West Brooksville, and in other structures.

Samuel M. Greene, then on the Colby College faculty, wrote in the *Magazine of Art* for 1947: "The Blue Hill Baptist Church is in great contrast to the academic refinement of the church on the other side of the town. Each church has a beauty that is quite its own. The Baptist Church may be a

BAPTIST CHURCH BLUEHILL ME.

Courtesy of Robert Sweetall

little more interesting because it is unique, while the Congregational follows more closely a conventional manner."

Lord's other churches show that he dared to be original. In the Brooklin Church he used a Gothic-like scroll and carved leaves. In the Sedgwick Church he placed a carving around the painted date "1838." Many people admire most the West Brooksville Church. The pediment, the entablature over the doors, and the stages of the tower each includes a series of three elements. The interior is as it was built by Lord. The nearby churchyard cemetery adds to the old-world atmosphere. The present steps do not follow the design and plan of the builder. The Ellsworth Congregational Church was designed and built by Lord. Its beautiful steeple, replaced in this century, is a county landmark.

Among Lord's papers are figures for wages paid him for his work on the Ellsworth Church:

To Thomas Lord

1846 to 138 1/2 days working on
meeting house $253.40
1847 to 214 1/2 days working on
meeting house $392.80
Four day making plans etc. $7.39
Going to Bangor to see about timber $3.00
Total $656.59

Lord built a house for his family not far from George Stevens's house. It is a Greek Revival house, correct in every line. The portico is like one in Deane's *Builder's Guide*. The interior has beautiful fireplaces. Some of the rooms are decorated with the Lord rosette. The Chase home, the second house beyond the Lord home, is most likely also the work of Thomas Lord.

Thomas Lord continued to build ships as well. For many years he was employed by George Stevens. The list of craft built in the days of Lord shows that the craft were varied. Brigs and barks, ships and schooners were built in Blue Hill yards. It is claimed that the *Magnolia*, built in Stevens's yard in 1833, was the first three-masted schooner ever launched.

Thomas Lord lived during the golden years of wooden ships. From 1840 to 1860 fifty-two ocean-going craft were built in Blue Hill. Some took granite to Atlantic coastal cities and New Orleans; some took lumber to southern ports and brought back cotton to northern mills; some took farm goods and staves to the Caribbean islands and brought back sugar and molasses.

Thomas Lord lived in Blue Hill when the harbor was crowded with shipping. August and the fall of 1830 may have been the high-water mark for Blue Hill as a port. I quote figures for only a few days:

August 6	5 SCHOONERS ARRIVED
August 7	2 SCHOONERS SAILED
August 9	2 SCHOONERS SAILED
Sept. 25	7 SCHOONERS, ALL HAILING FROM BOSTON SAILED
Nov. 27	7 SCHOONERS SAILED FROM BLUE HILL

Thomas Lord lived to see the decline of shipbuilding and shipping. An article in an Ellsworth paper for March 15, 1867, blamed the decline on the Civil War and the high tariff. The writer failed to realize that steam was winning out over sail; that English iron ships were winning out over American wooden craft.

Thomas Lord's ships and schooners are long since gone. But his beautiful houses and churches remain, reminders of a native builder of talent and originality.

27

The Longs of East Blue Hill

JOEL LONG WAS THE FIRST permanent settler on McHard's Stream. He came about 1812 to operate a sawmill built and owned by Daniel Spofford, who, as early as 1790, had a store and potash works at the Head-of-the-Bay. In a few years Long bought both the mill and land from Spofford and moved his wife and five children from Sedgwick to the mouth of the stream named for James McHard, one of the original proprietors of the town.

Joel Long prospered. He built for his family a large clapboarded house with brick ends. Using the power of the stream, he operated both a sawmill and a gristmill. Using the clay of the cove, he made bricks. In a meadow beside the bay he built ships: the *Two Sisters* in 1825, the *Venus* in 1836, and the *Randolph Martin* in 1842. In all, Joel and Joel Junior built eleven ships in the Long yard.

Few Blue Hill boys graduated from the local academy, but many Long boys did, and many went on to become teachers. Few Blue Hill men graduated from college, but

several Longs did: Charles Collins Long, Joel's son, graduated from Colby College; Charles Boardman Long, Joel's
grandson, went to the Eastern State Normal School; Edwin
Collins Long, another of Joel's grandsons, graduated from
Colby College; Herbert Long, a grandson of Joel, graduated
from the Newton Theological Seminary.

Numerous Longs became educated, ordained ministers,
and three became missionaries. Some of the men interested
in religious work as boys and young men had listened to the
preaching of the reform-minded Elder James Gilpatrick,
who preached in the Baptist Church at the Head-of-the-Bay.
Some were brought up by mothers who turned their sons'
thoughts to religion. Eliza Rogers, Joel's wife, was brought
up and educated in Boston. Lavinia Howard, James's wife,
was a bright and ambitious woman. Charles and Joel,
Junior, sons of the first Joel, married Hannah and Abigail
Friend of Sedgwick, who as children and young women
listened to the preaching of Daniel Merrill, a talented minister who spoke for missions and reform. For certain, Abigail
and Hannah caught some of the enthusiasm of Daniel
Merrill. They were two of the founders of the first church in
East Blue Hill.

The three of Joel Long's descendants who became missionaries were Charles Collins Long, born 1812, who did
missionary work in Washington County; Herbert C. Long,
born in 1887, who went as missionary to Bengal in India;
and a Eugene Stover, who was born in 1865 and went as
missionary to the Indians in the West.

James Long, Joel's youngest son, sought adventure by
going to California in search of gold. He kept a journal of his
1854 journey west. The diary, begun on March 11, starts
with the entry, "This day I took my departure from home to
the Golden State."

There were several delays on Long's journey. The first one was in Belfast where he had gone to take the steamboat the next day. The steamer was filled and so he had to wait for passage on March 25. He arrived in Boston and on April 4 set out for New York City, going first by boat and then by cart. In his diary Long described the departure of his steamer:

> At half past two a gun from the fore ship announced her departure. There were hurrahs, cheers, and waving of hats. Now she swings smoothly in her channel and veers eastward and shapes her course straight for the wide Atlantic.

The ship arrived at Nicaragua on April 15 after a stop at Kingston, Jamaica. The trip across Nicaragua was made by river boat and lake boat and then on foot. On the four-day trip Long saw monkeys and tropical birds. He wrote, "Nothing but my better half seemed wanting to make this a paradise."

But when James Long reached the harbor on the Pacific, he had a disappointment. This is the diary record for April 20:

> This morning a vast crowd of passengers collected on the beach to embark to California. All was crowd and hustle. It was clear that the steamer would not carry all the passengers. When the small boats came for the passengers, nothing but an officer on horse and armed men could keep the passengers from rushing and filling the boats. So great was the rush that parents and children were separated, parents on board and children on shore.

Baggage went without owners and was left without owners. About 150 passengers were left of which I was one. I saw no chance to embark without damage to person and property.

James Long adjusted well to the delay. The steamship company paid for his board and he earned money by carpenter work. He walked and read the Bible. On May 5 he boarded the steamer *Sierra Nevada*. He wrote, "Went on board between sunset and dark by slinging my baggage on my shoulder and wading into the water up to my waist." On May 20 he made the final entry in his journal: "Passed the Golden Gate about 1/2 past four. Tide running strong. Beautiful harbor, one of the best in the world."

James Long's stay in California was brief. He left no diary to tell of it and his journey home. But his days of adventure were not over. He enlisted to fight in the Civil War, as did his nephews Moses Long and Joel Closson. The nephews were

Bird's-eye View of East Blue Hill, Maine.

Courtesy of Robert Sweetall

killed in the war but James returned safely and spent the remainder of his days in East Blue Hill. He took great pride in seeing the hamlet of four houses become a village of sixty-seven homes, two stores, a Grange hall, an Ancient Order hall, a schoolhouse, a church, and a post office. James also took pride in having three of his sons build homes near him. Ed and Solon became storekeepers. Miles was a granite cutter. A fourth son, Alonzo, owned a home and a sawmill at the Head-of-the-Bay.

Before Miles settled down to cutting granite, he sought adventure in the Coast Guard. Miles Howard Long had always been teased about his name. So when he joined the Coast Guard, he chose to use the name Howard Long. Soon his shipmates were saying to him, "How Long, how long are you?" One day the Coast Guard boat came into East Blue Hill harbor. When the villagers recognized the East Blue Hiller aboard, they called out, "Hello, Miles, glad to see you." At once a jolly crewman called, "Now 'How Long,' we know how long you are. You are Miles Long."

George Long, son of Joel Junior, went west in 1857. He went first to California where he worked in a mine and then on a ranch. He soon moved to Oregon, where he lived in four different towns. In one he taught school and then became the superintendent of schools. In Oregon he married Nancy Rogers, and brought her back to Blue Hill.

The Longs were housebuilders. They built seven houses. Joel Junior's, is made of bricks from the Long brickyard. In 1989 three of the houses are still owned by descendants of Joel Long.

The Longs were able men, and none was more able than Ralph Long, born 1877, the great-grandson of Joel Long, who became a sea captain. He began his working years as a granite cutter and then became a crewman on an Ellsworth vessel that took kiln wood and bricks to nearby ports. He was twenty-four when he owned his first vessel, the *Maud S.*, built in Milbridge. With a crew of one, he carried freight from Portland to the seacoast towns of eastern Maine. After he sold the *Maud S.*, he commanded packets owned or leased by a marine broker in Portland. In 1905, he bought the *Jennie A. Stubbs,* a three-masted schooner that took granite to southern ports. In turn he commanded and owned the *Henry Chase* and the *Ben Hur* that for several years carried lumber and cordwood to Boston and New York. His last vessel was the *Seth Nyman,* which he operated between Rockland and Matinicus. This was one of the last "coasters" to operate in Maine waters.

After Ralph Long retired from the sea, he ran a sawmill and cut and sold wood. He built and repaired houses. He supported school and church. He saw to it that both his son and daughter had an education after high-school graduation. He took pride in being the great-grandson of Joel Long.

And then there was Herbert Long, one of the most ardent church supporters of all of Joel's descendants. In the late 1890s and early 1900s, he lived with his family on Roque Island, some two miles from the mainland of Washington County. He was the caretaker for the Gardener estate. Every Sunday morning, summer or winter, he and his family rowed or sailed to the nearest mainland church for Sunday school, where Herbert taught a class. They stayed for the church service. Then they sailed or rowed home for a late Sunday dinner.

The Longs have lived at McHard's Cove for nearly two hundred years. Their activities in the village, their going and their returning, give a continuity to the history of East Blue Hill.

28

John Edward Horton, Miner and Soldier

JOHN EDWARD HORTON, born in Blue Hill in 1829, was the grandson of Joshua Horton, one of the first settlers. He grew up on the farm cleared by his grandfather. He was one of five brothers, only one of whom lived out his days in his native town.

Three of the four brothers felt the pull of the sea. Josiah went to sea from 1840 to 1845. He then gave up being a sailor and became a trucker in Boston and then a dairy farmer in Somerville. William Horton made numerous trips to the Caribbean. He died in Philadelphia in 1848 from a disease caught in Havana. George Horton was drowned at sea in 1845 when the Blue Hill schooner *Purveyor* struck a shoal and went down with only one survivor.

John Edward, the youngest brother, felt the pull of gold. In the early 1850s he went to California to mine. Six of his letters survive. They show that he was homesick and longed for a letter from home; that he was a successful miner; that he hoped to buy a farm in the West. His letters also show that he was a man of energy. Two letters that he wrote to his brother Josiah make good reading:

Poor Man's Creek Sept. 9th, 1854

Dear brother it has been a long time since I have had a letter from you. I thought that I would not write until I did get one but I have been waiting for one these last ten months in vain. The last letter that I had from you was dated last November and the last one that I had from home was dated a year ago this last August. I sent you a check for one hundred dollars last February and I wish you would let me know whether you got it or not. I have been in good health this summer and have been making very good wages but the water has failed now and we cannot make any thing until water comes again which will be about the middle of November. Two of my partners have sold out and gone home. They had about twenty five hundred dollars a piece but I shall stop here this winter. We have bought our winter's provisions—flour for ten cents a pound— ham 30 cents—bacon 26 cents—potatoes 8 cents— onions 12 cents—and other things in proportion which is very cheap for the mountains. Wages are very low in California now. You can hire plenty of men in the valley for three dollars and they board themselves. But wages are a little better here. Part of the miners are doing very well and some have a hard time to make their board. You may ask when I am coming home. That is a hard question to answer. I have made fifteen hundred dollars and have made it all within the past year and have as good show for another year. I have not seen nor heard from any of the Bluehillers out here since I have been here. Be sure and write as soon as you get this and write all of the news and about all the folks that I am acquainted with. Give my love to Louisa and Elizabeth and all inquiring friends. From your affectionate brother.

J. E. Horton

P. S. Direct your letters to Marysville in the care of Everts and Co. express Poor Man's Creek Plumas County.

Poor Man's Creek July 7th, 1855

I received your letter dated the first of March and was glad to hear that you had moved into the country for I think that you will enjoy yourselves a great deal more than you would in the city. I expect that Louisa is trying her skill in making butter and cheese. I wish I had some of it here to try my skill in eating it. I think I could do as much as any man in that line of business. I am engaged in the hog and poultry business. I have three partners; we have two hogs and five hens. It is a very good business but no profit. I am still at mining; doing very well but not as well as I expected. The claim cost me $1150.00 but I would not take what I gave for it. The miners are doing very well about here. There has been a good many gone home from here this year past, but there is a good many come back. They cannot stand the Maine liquor law. We have a division of the Sons of Temperance formed last week with twenty members. There is not more than half of the liquor drank here now as there was last year. California is reforming very fast. We have got a law against gambling and you do not see any gambling now in the stores and bar rooms. There was a minister preached here last Sunday — the first one for over a year. You may think that we are heathens and you would be about right for they make holiday of Sunday. The merchants sell more goods then any other day and the bar keepers more whiskey. I was to American valley and spent the fourth. It is eighteen miles from here. There was an oration in the forenoon, a bull fight in the afternoon, a ball at night. There was about forty ladies there which is a good many for the mountains. It is a valley about five miles long from one to two wide and very good farming land. There is one man that has over a hundred acres of grain. In my last letter I wrote that I should come home this fall but it is uncertain now. If I sell out, I may come home but that is uncertain. I had a letter from father dated in April. Write as soon as you get this.

J. E. Horton

John Edward never owned a farm in the West. He returned to Blue Hill, where in April of 1860 he married Laura Webber. The couple went to Massachusetts to live, likely to be near Josiah Horton. When he enlisted in August of 1862, he gave his residence as North Somerville and his occupation as milkman. He was an infantry man of Company E of the 39th Massachusetts Regiment.

There is no record of his war service before August 1864. His diary and a recollection written by his friend John F. Locke tell of the troubled months starting with mid-August

1864. Horton and Locke were among 1,800 Union soldiers captured by Confederate forces fighting in Virginia. The prisoners were marched from Petersburg to Libby Prison in Richmond. Locke wrote an account of their first days in the prison:

The next day the whole 1800 were escorted out of town about two miles that we might take the cars for Richmond. Three hardtacks (the first food received from our captors' hands) were given us to make us hungry and that we might enjoy our excursion. The sound of the battle in progress (the 21st) on the same ground where we were captured was plainly heard, and we could but wish that the results might be more favorable than those of the 19th. Towards the last of the afternoon we arrived in Richmond and as we alighted from the coal cars we were told that only one hotel in the place could accommodate us and the one was "The Libby" and, as we were strangers in town and might wish to look round a little, we were escorted through some of the principal streets. Finally the procession brought in up in front of Libby and we were stowed away in it; thus in nine of its rooms were packed 1800 men. We spent a portion of our time in examining our new quarters, the walls of which were covered with the names of former fellow sufferers. Here we received our first half loaf of cornbread which was not so bad in quality as it was in quantity. Then came orders from the Prison Inspector, Dick Turner, to hand over all moneys to him for safe keeping, and some unsophisticated ones obeyed, having their names duly registered, but I have not heard that Turner gave any receipt or that anything ever came back. After a very uncom-

fortable night, owing to our crowded condition, we
were glad to see the morning and soon afterwards, we
were taken across the street (Carey) to Penberton
prison and distributed in its rooms in squads of twenty-
five. Turner soon came in and, in his insolent, arrogant
style, ordered us to strip ourselves that our clothes
might be searched for valuables.

Our wallets, watches, jackknives, rings and everything of comfort or value that was not absolutely
necessary was gathered into a heap and Turner, with
greedy eye, not only inspected but appropriated. At
the end of a long half hour we were permitted to dress
and then were conducted back to Libby, and other
squads followed, the procession continuing till well
into the next day, everyone pretty well thoroughly
plucked. After all, many of the cunning Yankees were
able to circumvent the rebels, since bills of large de-
nominations were hidden in such queer places as ears,
mouth and hair, thus enabling the possessor to procure
needed comforts in coming days.

In a few weeks Locke, Horton, and others were moved
from Libby Prison to a prison in Salisbury, North Carolina.
John Edward's diary gives a grim and poignant picture of
prison life:

Tues., August 23 — Slept first rate. Wash up and eat
breakfast. They put part of us into another building
opposite; take our names, number of regiment and
where we were born, then search us, take our haver-
sacks, etc. Give us rations about 1 P.M. take us to Belle
Isle; there are a little over 3,000 of us here. We are
divided into squads of 30; Ladd is our Sergeant.

Thurs., 25 — Brown is at work, outside, helping the

cook; get our rations from across the river; attend prayer meeting.

Mon., 29 — About 2100 came from Libby, of the Second Corps; they were taken the 25th at Reams Station; am sorry to see them.

Tues., 30 — Provisions are very high; small loaves of bread are $5.00; sugar $12.00; onions $1.00; apples $2.00 and $3.00. For $1.00 we get one-fourth of a loaf of bread, a small piece of bacon and a little bean soup, just enough to keep us alive.

Sat., Sept. 3 — They have stopped the speculation in corn bread. The Lieutenant says all of it is ours and he will see that we get it. Write a short letter to Laura; fear she may not get my letters; there is a prayer meeting every night. I attend and hope they may do me good.

Sun., October 16 — Sell my ring for $60. Confederate money and buy a blanket for $40. Am sorry to part with the ring, but the blanket will do me more good. A number die every day.

Thurs., 20 — Our rations are bread, molasses and rice soup.

Thurs., 27 — 500 more prisoners arrive from Richmond; they were taken in the Valley and belong to the Sixth, Eighth and Nineteenth Corps.

Fri., 28 — Twenty-seven died in the last twenty-four hours; it is sad to see men suffer and die off in this way; my health is still good; have nothing but rice to-day.

Sat., Nov. 5 — A number take the oath of allegiance to old Jeff. The Union boys hooted them and kicked one so that he died. Creedon took the oath.

Tues., 8 — To-day is Election; wish I were home to vote for Old Abe. Get no bread; or meat, but about a quart of rice soup; feel hungry and weak.

Wed., 9 — Get some bread; went sixty hours on a

little over a quart of poor rice soup. Felt weak and faint, but feel better since getting some bread; from twenty-five to fifty die every day.

Fri., 11 — Get bread, meat and soup, but no salt in soup. Or no meat, there is none in camp.

Sat., 12 — The long roll was beat three times last night. Someone stoned the guard; have only nine months more to serve.

Mon., 14 — The coldest night of the season thus far; sell a pair of socks for $5.00 Confederate money and buy some salt at $1.50 a pint.

Wed., 16 — Rained a little in the night: The papers say Abe is elected sure.

Fri., 18 — Help take Allen of the Fourth New Hampshire to the hospital; think he cannot live long. It is sad sight to see how the men are dying off.

Sun., 20 — This does not seem like the Sabbath; little Orren is seventeen months old; wish I were at home to see him.

Mon., 21 — Rheumatism troubles me some; Allen of the Fourth New Hampshire died last night.

Sat., 26 — Got a letter from Laura dated Oct. 2nd, and another this afternoon dated August 27th; they are all well; am very glad to hear from them. Phillips (E) died last night.

Mon., 28 — the Rebs count every division at the same time to stop flankers; have an attack of diarrhea.

Tues., 29 — 370 take oath of allegiance to Jeff and go into the rebel army. Short rations and so many dying urge them to this step; diarrhea a little worse.

Wed., 30 — Am some better; this is my thirty-fifth birthday; hope to be able to spend my next at home. It is a real Indian Summer day. P. Merril of the First Massachusetts Calvry died in our tent. The chimney in the hospital fell, killing one man and wounding several.

Thurs., Dec. 1 — A fine day for the first of winter; am much better; sold my rations and bought some bread flour; Locke gave me some pills.

Fri., 2 — It is just fifteen weeks since I was taken prisoner, am in strong hopes of being exchanged soon; feel about well.

Sun., 4 — Could hear the church bells and it made me feel homesick; how I wish I could be at home with my wife and boy.

Sat., 10 — Stormed all night; about three inches of snow fell; a cold, bad night for us prisoners, but I managed to keep warm. Gorham (E) died this morning about two o'clock; he was sick but a short time.

Mon., 12 — It froze hard, very cold for those who have no blankets. General Winder and some other rebel officers were here to inspect the condition of the prisoners. Am some better to-day, got wheat flour.

Fri., 16 — A few more Yankee prisoners came in, three of the Thirty-ninth, one (Burns) from "B" and one Hemenway from "K" captured last Sunday (11), near Weldon, sorry to see them here, but glad to hear from the regiment.

Thurs., 22 — Drew bread, soup and syrup, no meat for a long time.

Sun., 25 — Cloudy, with raw, cool wind, a dull Christmas for me. We got one-half a loaf of bread and a little rice soup for our Christmas dinner, breakfast and supper; wish I were at home, but see little signs of an exchange.

Wed., 28 — Tipton was elected our squad sergeant in place of White (deposed) our tent run for Haun, but he got beat; think we have a good sergeant. Rumor says there is to be a general exchange of prisoners the first of January; hope it is true.

Thurs., 29 — Rained quite hard all night and our tent leaked some. Do not feel very well but hope I shall not be sick.

Fri., 30 — A cool, dull day. Have the diarrhea quite bad, but am in hopes to get rid of it soon. John Locke gave me some pills.

Sat., 31 — Rained about all day; comes on cold and snows some. Had the diarrhea very bad all night; a cold, dull disagreeable day for the very last of 1864. It looks like a dark prospect ahead for us prisoners, but I am in hopes to be exchanged soon; so the story runs.

Sun., Jan. 1, 1865 — A fine pleasant morning but cool. It does not look like a very happy New Year for me, but am in hopes to get out of this soon. God grant it may be a happy and pleasant one to my wife and boy. Am a little better this morning.

John Edward Horton died on January 6, 1865. His body was brought to Blue Hill for burial. Laura, with her only child, Orrin, returned to Maine to live. Orrin never felt the pull of the sea. Nor did he hear the call of California. He became a builder of homes, stores, and lodge halls. The structures that he built were foursquare and sturdy.

29

Soldiers for the Union

MAINE CONTRIBUTED ABOUT 70,000 MEN to fight in the Civil War. John J. Pullen in his superb book *The Twentieth Maine* wrote that three motives influenced men to volunteer: imitation of friends and relatives who were enlisting; love for the Union; desire to get away from the humdrum life of the farms.

The last reason did not influence the numerous Blue Hill sailors who volunteered. They had already left home; they were already leading exciting lives. Thomas Osgood of Blue Hill wrote that in his eleven years of going to sea before 1861, he had visited every major United States city on the Atlantic coast, made numerous trips to the West Indies and Brazil, and in 1853 had gone on a ship that took supplies to the English army fighting Russia on the Crimean Peninsula.

Sewall Snowman, another Blue Hill sailor, had enlisted in the navy before war broke out. He visited Montevideo, Cuba, and Egypt. In 1861 he was in Charleston, South Carolina. He wrote this account of what happened:

In the fall and winter of 1860–61 I spent time in Charleston, South Carolina and was present at the State Convention held on December 20th, 1860, when the resolution was passed declaring the state of South Carolina forever separated from the Union. While I was there, six other states separated from the Union. In January, 1861, just before I left, a posse of men dragged four pieces of cannon to the pier of the New York Mail Service and when she was abreast the pier, the mob ordered the captain to haul down the Stars and Stripes, or they would fire. Their demands were complied with and the steamer was allowed to come in to the pier, which was the first open, wanton insult to the flag. Although it was late in January, the atmosphere was too hot for my comfort being reeking with treason. I took passage in the last northern vessel in port bound north and in three days was in New York City.

Volunteers were farmers, carpenters, fishermen, quarrymen, and granite cutters. Some were coopers, blacksmiths, shipbuilders, and undertakers. The volunteers numbered a teacher, a miner, a barkeeper, and two lighthouse keepers. Two volunteers had gone west to dig gold and returned poor. One volunteer listed his occupation as "hunter." That man was Warren Clay. He supported his claim by listing the animals he had killed in the winter of 1851–52: thirty-seven deer, one bear, five wildcats, one lynx, several mink, one otter, nine foxes, and several coons. It comes as no surprise that Mr. Clay became a Union sharpshooter.

The Gazetteer of Maine states, "Blue Hill furnished 196 men in defence of the Union." The early volunteers served in the Fourth, Sixth, Seventh, Twelfth, Thirteenth, and Fourteenth Maine regiments. Most served in the infantry. But there were cavalrymen, scouts, wagoneers, guards of ammunition trains, sharpshooters, and musicians.

The youngest enlistee from Blue Hill was Ambrose Stover, aged thirteen years one month. Albino Carter, Stephen Wescott, James Gray, George Clay, Robert Betell, and Eben Hale all served for three years. Two men who came to Blue Hill after 1866 had served in the Army of Occupation. Those men were Charles Appel, who served for forty-six months, and Harrison Tripp, who was in the service for fifty-five months. The former was the manager of East Blue Hill's "Pittsburgh Quarry" which in the 1870s sent granite to build the post office in Pittsburgh.

Until 1863, each state was responsible for raising troops for the war. When Lincoln gave a call for a certain number of men, each state was notified as to the size of its quota. A state in turn notified each town and city as to the size of its quota. Men were expected to enlist. Blue Hill's enrollment officer was Joseph Hinckley. Like other towns, Blue Hill paid a bounty to those who enlisted. When Hinckley could not find enough volunteers in Blue Hill, he went to towns that paid a smaller bounty than Blue Hill and he usually found enough men to fill his town's quota. Blue Hill's bounty was at first fifty dollars, but it went up until it was three hundred dollars. Blue Hill's town records show that the town from time to time raised money to help the families of those in the service. Two or three times, the widow or mother of a man killed in battle was given money. By the close of the war, Blue Hill had paid $18,445 in bounties. The national government paid a hundred-dollar bounty. The state of Maine also paid a bounty, the amount of which increased as the years went by. The volunteer-bounty system encouraged desertions. A volunteer could desert, re-enlist, and so collect a second bounty. One Midwesterner "bounty-jumped" thirty-two times.

The *Ellsworth American* did all it could to encourage enlistments. In the issue of November 8, 1861, is this advice:

Let Old Hancock arouse from her lethargy and send forth strong hands and warm Union hearts to battle for Right and the Union. There should be Union meetings in every town. This is a terribly earnest Rebellion.

Blue Hill held Union meetings before there was any urging from the *American*. The *Ellsworth American* reported the meeting of April 1861:

A flag was raised on South Street. The greatest enthusiasm prevailed and cheer after cheer rent the air, showing that the spirit of '76 still lives. There was the firing of guns and cheers for Lincoln, General Scott and Major Anderson. There were groans for that traitor Jefferson Davis.

Evidently not everyone in Blue Hill agreed with the South Street patriots. Someone cut down the flag raised in North Blue Hill. But Blue Hill prided herself on being a strong Union town. Townspeople called the war "the Great Rebellion." They denounced the pro-Southern *Bangor Democrat*, published by Marcellus Emery. (Before the war was over, a mob of Bangor Unionists destroyed Emery's press.) Blue Hill people were alarmed when a gang of toughs, likely "Seceshs," attacked a battery in Castine and plundered homes in Stockton Springs. Blue Hill people frowned on Southern sympathizers, called "Copperheads."

Throughout the war Blue Hill ladies sent articles to the Sanitary Commission for distribution to the soldiers. The *Ellsworth American* for October 11, 1861, gave a list of items that the commission desired: stockings, blankets, quilts, woolen or flannel wrappers, undershirts and drawers, bed gowns, small pillows for wounded limbs, slippers, delicacies such as farina, arrowroot, cocoa, and dried fruits.

As patriotic ardor increased, so did the dislike for England. English-built ships, owned by the Confederacy, preyed upon New England shipping. The *Tallahassee* seized and destroyed four fishing schooners off Matinicus Rock. The *Alabama* seized and destroyed four Hancock County fishing schooners. Off New York, the *Alabama* overtook a Blue Hill ship with Moses Johnson as captain. The crew was taken to the *Alabama* and the Blue Hill craft destroyed. Captain and crew were eventually landed in Liverpool.

The year 1863 was cruel for both civilians and soldiers. Prices rose. Bacon was $6.50 a pound, beans $35 to $50 a barrel, potatoes $12 to $20 a bushel, lard $17.50 a pound, and molasses $60 a barrel. Blue Hill people depended upon the sea, the clam flats, the brooks, and their gardens for their food. There were military defeats. Enthusiasm for the war and faith in victory faltered. The passing of the Conscription Act of 1863 divided public opinion and led to violence. The law was necessary because the states were not providing enough troops to win the war. The Conscription Act gave the federal government the power to enroll all males between the ages of twenty and forty-five. Draftees were to serve for three years. Lincoln called for 300,000 men.

There were legal ways by which a draftee could avoid service in the army. He could pay a $300 commutation fee. This excused him from service until another draft. He could hire a substitute. Hiring a substitute meant permanent exemption. Maine men could hire a substitute from Delaney and Yates, an Augusta firm that secured immigrants, underage men, and overage men to go as substitutes. One

Blue Hill man sent a neighbor's young son as his substitute. There was also an illegal way to avoid the draft. A man could leave home. Thousands of "skedaddlers" fled to the deep woods, Aroostook, or Canada. There was a painful way to avoid going into the service. A man could mutilate himself by cutting off toes or fingers. At least one Blue Hill man did mutilate himself and bore to the end of days the ugly name of Copperhead. This item appeared in a local paper:

> Those drafted persons who have knocked out their front teeth to procure exemption, are informed that they will be accepted in the cavalry, where front teeth are not needed to bite off cartridges.

The federal draft made the war unpopular in Maine. In the year 1863, only about 2,500 Maine men entered the service as substitutes, draftees, or volunteers. In the year 1864 forty-seven Blue Hill men were drafted. Probably many of them secured substitutes.

Blue Hill men served in nearly every area of fighting. They fought at Second Bull Run, Antietam, Fredericksburg, Chancellorsville, Gettysburg, the Wilderness, Spotsylvannia, and Petersburg. One rode with Sheridan; two were with Banks on his Red River campaign; two fought to take Fort Hudson on the Mississippi.

Some of Blue Hill's soldiers were killed in battle; some died from wounds. But many of the wounded lived and returned home. George Clay was one of the fortunate. He wrote an account of his experiences as a wounded soldier:

> I was in the campaign in the Wilderness and Spotsyl-vannia, up to the 12th of May, 1864, when I was

wounded in the face and neck. I was soon taken off the field and my wounds were dressed. The next day I started to ride in an army wagon to Fredricksburg but I was so badly shaken up that I got out and walked with the team. Stopped at Fredricksburg one night and started for Belle Plain Landing on foot with a train. I arrived at the Landing on the same day and found a steamer waiting . By this time I had got pretty hungry, for my jaw was broken and a bullet hole through my neck. Under the conditions, to chew hardtack was out of the question, so that for the last few days, my diet was mostly coffee.

I had the good fortune to fall in with a gentleman who was looking after the interests of those who were Masons, and at once I was taken to a tent near the wharf where I was given all the milk punch that I could drink. If there was ever a time when I wished I could hold more, that was the time! We arrived in Washington some time in the night, and the first man that I met when I stepped off the train was Captain Benjamin F. Buck of my own company's medical corps. I was taken to a hospital the next day and sent to the Saterlee United States General Hospital, near Philadelphia, where I remained until August 30th, 1864.

George Clay returned to Blue Hill and lived a long and prosperous life. He was active in church and civic affairs and a trustee of Blue Hill Academy. Though he escaped violent death on the battlefield, he was killed when dynamite exploded in the granite yard of which he was the foreman.

When Lincoln was assassinated, Republicans and War Democrats united to mourn the slain president and a serv-

ice was held in the Blue Hill Baptist Church. Ladies decorated the interior of the church with black and placed a
motto above the pulpit — "God reigneth. Let the earth
tremble." Pastor Bowker of the Congregational Church
spoke for three-quarters of an hour and Pastor Eveleth of
the Baptist Church spoke for fifteen minutes.

The finale at the close of the war was a grand parade in
Washington, D. C. At least four Blue Hill men were in the
parade: Alfred, Rodney and Thomas Osgood were there,
along with Sewall Snowman. In 1861, Snowman was angry
when he saw South Carolina secede from the Union. In
1865, he must have been proud when he marched in the
parade that celebrated a reunited Union.

Generation to Generation

Courtesy of Robert Sweetall

30

Abbey Fulton, Career Woman

ABBEY M. FULTON WAS A TRAVELER and a doctor. Her contemporaries wrote of her charm and beauty, her strong will, and her commanding presence. One of them wrote: "No one ever picked up a gauntlet thrown down by her who did not find her a foeman worthy of his steel."

She was born in Brooksville and educated at Blue Hill Academy. The Academy aimed to give students an education based on Latin and Greek, with a smattering of science, geology, biology, and chemistry. At Blue Hill Academy a course in navigation was given for the benefit of young men who hoped to go to sea.

Perhaps young Abbey stayed at the Blue Hill House or boarded with a local family. She must have made friends with the Hinckleys, Osgoods, Cloughs, and Peters, who were her contemporaries.

We do know that she made one very good friend. That

friend was Dr. Alexander Fulton. On January 14, 1849, Abbey and the doctor were married. It is safe to assume that Dr. Fulton was anticipating the marriage in 1848. In that year, he had built a brig, *The Bride*.

The Fultons went to live at "The Traveler's Home," now the Holt House. There Dr. Fulton had his office. When Thomas Jefferson Napoleon Holt, the owner of the inn, brought home a bride in 1852, he ceased to run an inn but he allowed the Fultons to live in his home. Holt, usually called Napoleon, was a painter and paper-hanger. His bride was Clarissa Peters. Young Abbey and young Clarissa probably became good friends. Abbey never had children but she must have taken pleasure in little Alice and Clara Holt.

Living in the Holt home, Abbey's thoughts must have turned to the sea and traveling. When she stepped out of doors, she heard the sound of saws and hammers from George Stevens's shipyard. Next door in the brick block that he had built about 1835, Jonah Holt had a store and an office from which he managed his affairs as a merchant and shipbuilder. Abbey must have known many Blue Hill men who went to sea. She must have known Mrs. James Roundy Candage who had six sons who were lost at sea or died in foreign ports.

Abbey's thoughts also likely turned to reform. The anti-slavery movement was strong in the 1850s, and several Blue Hill families went to Kansas to fight the extension of slavery into that territory. The *Ellsworth American* was filled with articles against the use of liquor. The articles "The Drunkard's Wife" and "The Drunkard's Son" were especially poignant. In the 1840s, several people in Blue Hill had licenses to sell liquor. But, by 1858, by a vote of 59 to 25, the voters prohibited the sale of liquor in Blue Hill.

Reformers did not hesitate to aim a few rocks at the sale

of tobacco, too. In an *Ellsworth American* article is this statement: "The victims of tobacco are thirsty the world over." A man wrote: "The use of tobacco is a serious hindrance to religious growth, enjoyment, and usefulness. It is a needless and wicked waste of means."

Young Abbey must have been excited by the news of secession in 1861, proud that Blue Hill was so fiercely pro-Union, and saddened by the number of Hancock County men who were killed in the Civil War. In the last year of the war, Doctor Fulton represented Blue Hill in the legislature. Perhaps Abbey went to Augusta with him. Perhaps she stayed at home, doled out medicine to his patients herself, and made a few house calls. By 1865, Abbey had decided herself to become a doctor.

My aunt, Hannah Wood Howard, was Abbey Fulton's contemporary. In the late 1860s and early 1870s, Aunt Hannah, her husband, and four sons lived in the Friend's Corner neighborhood. Aunt Hannah was a great storyteller. She told true stories, she told stories that she had read, and she told stories that were a product of her imagination.

One of Aunt Hannah's true stories was about Abbey Fulton's return from a trip she took to Paris. Abbey had bought and wore a Parisian corset. Her figure was the talk of the town. But she also brought from Paris the recipe for a French sweet. She advised her fellow Baptists of the Ladies Aid that she would bring samples of the delicacy to the next meeting of the society. She said she would sell recipes for the French sweet at the price of ten cents each. The proceeds were to be added to the funds of the ladies' group.

Aunt Hannah was one of the ladies who went to the meeting where the French import made its Blue Hill debut. She told a long story of the meeting. She described the parlor in which the meeting was held. She told how the dining table was laden with gleaming glass and flowered Haviland. Abbey made a dramatic entry into the front hall and then into the parlor. She wore a Parisian gown and swung a large basket covered with a linen tray cloth. She removed the cloth, handed the basket to her hostess, and bade her make the rounds of the room with the basket. In the basket there were cream puffs, large and crusty, and oozing with rich custard. Later each lady was served a cream puff. There were ohs and ahs of pleasure and a lively sale of the recipes.

In the late 1860s or early 1870s Dr. and Mrs. Fulton moved to Ellsworth. Then Abbey went to New York and studied medicine. She next attended a women's medical school in Boston. She returned to Ellsworth and practiced medicine with her husband. In a few years she went to Paris for further study. In 1874 she was in London where she was a clinical assistant to Dr. Prothero Smith, one of the famous doctors of her day. He had founded Soho Hospital for Women where Abbey practiced under eminent surgeons.

After Dr. Abbey returned to Ellsworth, she resumed work with her husband and made a specialty of treating women and children. In 1878, she again went to Europe for study. Evidently the Fulton team did well financially. In 1888 the Drs. Fulton started a summer home in Southwest Harbor.

But Dr. Alexander Fulton died in 1888. Abbey chose to have him buried in Blue Hill. She had placed on his burial lot a massive monument cut of Blue Hill granite and, in her husband's memory, she gave a clock to the town of Blue Hill. The clock was placed in the belfry of the Baptist Church, where for a century it has ticked away the hours.

Dr. Abbey Fulton gradually withdrew from the practice of medicine and devoted her entire time to good causes and reform. She maintained a summer home in Southwest Harbor and a winter home in Washington, D.C. She supported the cause of woman suffrage and was a strong supporter of the Women's Christian Civic League. She was a charter member of Sorosis, the first women's club founded in the United States. She was a member of the select Washington group known as Wi-mo-dau-sis Club. The club took its name from the first letters of the words *wife, mother, daughter,* and *sister.* She became a close friend of Sarah Hale, editor and reformer.

But I feel sure she never forgot Blue Hill.

31

Milford Grindle,
District School Agent

MY GREAT-GRANDFATHER GRINDLE was the school agent in the Granite District, Number Seven, in the 1870s. It was his duty to spend the school funds allotted the rural district by the town, to hire the teacher, to see that the schoolhouse was kept in good repair, and to secure the wood for the big iron stove that warmed the classroom.

I wonder why the selectmen so often chose my great-grandfather for the job of district agent. They did not choose him because he was a good disciplinarian. Indeed, in this respect he was notoriously lax in spite of his bluster. His grandchildren, driven by shouts from his workshop, returned to play at the bench after their grandfather went into the kitchen. Hens, scared from the garden by threats of violence, came from their bush sanctuary after their owner had passed. Cows and pigs, oxen and horses grew accustomed to his corrective shouts. They soon learned that neither child nor beast suffered violence from his hand because, as my grandmother used to say, "Father roars like a lion but he acts like a dove."

Great-grandfather was not selected because he was an intellectual man. Perhaps he was chosen because his little paving quarry was the one thriving enterprise of the neighborhood or because he lived near the schoolhouse and had grandchildren to send to the school.

The big boys in the 1870s often gave trouble. My grandmother, who was then unmarried and was at home caring for the younger children, recalled that one problem involved the "manufacture" of the cordwood. It was customary to have five or six cords of wood hauled to the school yard in February, sawed in April by the men of the neighborhood, and then split and wheeled into the shed by the boys of the school during the months of September and October. The splitting and wheeling were usually done at odd moments during recess and noontime and so worked no hardship on the pupils.

But this particular fall the boys declared that their recesses and noon hours were for playing and not for working. The teacher's urging and their parents' bidding brought no results. So late in October Great-grandfather turned to strategy. Every noontime when he returned to the quarry, he halted his yoke of oxen by the roadside, took his axe from the drag, and, while Bright and Broad cropped the grass, he split the wood. He spoke pleasantly to the children and he paused to watch the big boys at their game of baseball. When a good hit was made, he gave a shout of approval. For several weeks the schoolyard was a noisy place at noontime with blows of the axe often drowning out the shouts of children at play.

My grandmother scolded her father: "You ought not to

split wood in your noon hour. It makes me mad clear through to think of you working while those lazy big boys are playing."

"Now don't get riled, Ellie," he said. "I won't have to do but a little more. The boys will finish the job and wheel the wood into the shed."

Soon Great-grandfather went to the county seat. He made a number of purchases and one of them was a baseball bat. The next day when he went to the schoolyard to do his stint at the woodpile, he gave the bat to the boys and remarked, "I've noticed that you players are using a cracked bat. Here is one that is considerably better. Take it and see if you can knock a home run."

That was the last day that the school agent saw service at the schoolhouse woodpile. The boys organized a Saturday splitting and wheeling bee. By nightfall the wood had been split and wheeled into the shed. A few weeks later when the Grindle family returned from a day's trip to Sedgwick, they found that the remnants of wood in their own yard had, during their absence, been wheeled into the shed and neatly stacked.

"A boy is like a calf and I never knew a critter that wouldn't respond to a kittle of warm mash and molasses," was Great-grandfather's comment.

A few years later a greater crisis than unsplit wood faced the agent of Number Seven. The large boys of the school, encouraged by snickering girls, beset the teacher with tricks so numerous and so annoying that master after master refused to teach the Granite School.

The school at McHard's Village was also beset with unruly boys. There, the big students forcibly carried the master to the bridge over the tidal stream and, at low tide, dropped him onto the mud flats. Great-grandfather and the

McHard's agent met to talk over their problems and they decided to drive to Bangor, to hire "out-of-town teachers" capable of taming the children of their districts.

The agents drove to Bangor with the Grindle horse, Old Gyp; spent one day teacher-hunting; and on the third day, a cold November Friday with clouds that threatened snow, returned with a teacher for the East Blue Hill school and with a box of belongings for the District Seven teacher who was to arrive shortly.

Great-grandfather was strangely silent about the new teachers who had been hired. In reply to his daughters' queries he did say that they were cousins, that they did not look alike, and that they did not have the same names. Further questioning brought out the fact that the East Blue Hill teacher's name was Prouty and that his cousin's name was Ewer.

Teacher Prouty arrived on Sunday. He soon won a township reputation and he won it in one forenoon of activity. The gentle-spoken master proved to be a prize fighter. The whippings that he gave the local bullies inaugurated a long term of peace at the school.

The children at the Granite School were awed by the tales of Mr. Prouty's powers as a disciplinarian and they looked forward fearfully to meeting his cousin.

But on Wednesday their fears were displaced by amazement. When they went to school expecting to be challenged by a grim and brawny fighter, they were welcomed by a slender young woman with a withered arm.

Miss Ewer called the school to order, wrote the name of each pupil on the board, and asked the big boys to unpack boxes. What treasures the boxes held — maps, reading charts with pictures, colored chalk, a great globe — such things as the children had never seen.

One box held books on the stars and the sea, books on sewing and painting; it held books of adventure yarns and books of fairy tales. "We shall have a reading room in the corner," promised the teacher to the bemused pupils.

That was not the only promise that Miss Ewer made. The first day was taken up with plans and promises. She made plans for a spelling bee and a debate in which the students of the Granite School would challenge Mr. Prouty's students. She promised to instruct the larger boys in navigation in an after-school class and to teach painting to a Saturday afternoon class. She assigned the older children as "practice teachers" to help the little pupils while she was busy with the middle grades. She kept the big boys so interested that they never thought of pranks and mischief.

And the interest outlasted the first day. Never had the school house buzzed with such activity. It was used at night, thanks to Great-grandfather who bought four bracket lamps for the classroom. Grandmother suspected that the lamps were bought with paving money rather than the school money, but she did not complain. She herself went back to school for painting lessons and for the Friday evening writing classes.

When the schools closed in June the teaching cousins returned to Bangor. Neither returned to the classroom. Mr. Prouty became a professional fighter; Miss Ewer became a housewife.

But Addie Ewer is still spoken of in the Friend's Corner neighborhood though the schoolhouse has been closed for almost a century. I like to think about Addie Ewer's success in quelling mutiny in the classroom.

I like also to think of Great-grandfather's success as district agent. As long as he lived, people used to ask him, "How did it happen, Mr. Grindle, that you dared to hire a one-armed girl to deal with a school of unruly children?"

He always gave the same answer, "I was looking for a teacher to win the scholars, not to whip them. I knew that when a teacher can catch a young one's interest, she won't have to cudgel him."

32

Augustus Hinckley, Adventurer

"IF GUS HINCKLEY HAD LIVED IN THE MIDDLE AGES, he would have gone on the Crusades." This was Father's comment about the older brother of his friend Wallace Hinckley. Father and the men of his generation liked to talk about the young Hinckley who had enlisted in the United States Navy in 1898 and the army in 1899, then had fought in the Boer War and had seen service in both World War I and II. He lived his civilian life in cities where he was an organizer for the Independent Workers of the World (IWW), which aimed to organize unskilled laborers. He never returned home to Blue Hill after the death of his mother in 1909.

Father and his contemporaries discussed why a man with Hinckley and Peters blood was a soldier of fortune and a labor organizer. One man suggested that a quarrel with his father turned Augustus to adventure and radicalism. Another had the unlikely theory that Gus felt rejected because he was born in Conway, New Hampshire, and spent his early years there. I have another theory: As a young teenager, Gus listened to the Civil War stories told by his two Peters great-uncles who had fought in the war. One of the uncles admitted to Gus's mother that his war stories were always about the glory and excitement of war, never about its misery and boredom.

William Hinckley, Gus's nephew, some eighty years after the Spanish-American War, made a typed copy of the journal that Gus kept while he was in the Philippines helping to put down the rebellion that followed the American occupation of the islands. I draw upon this copy for information about the war experiences of one of Blue Hill's most adventurous sons.

He had his first taste of adventure when he was seventeen years old. Enlisted in the navy, he served a few months in the war against Spain. But his search for further adventure in the Philippines was at first checked by his father, Eugene Hinckley. A piece in the *Bangor Daily Commercial* for June 1899 tells the story:

Gus Hinckley, an 18 year old giant from Bluehill, doesn't hanker so much for a life on the field of Mars as he did; his father came up from Bluehill after him on Monday, and found him here ready to enlist in the army of the Philippines.

Young Hinckley, who, though but a boy in years, is a giant in size and weight, served in the navy in part of the Spanish War; during part of the war, he was on the famous auxiliary cruiser *Yankee*. When he returned to the peaceful vales of Hancock county, things looked different than at the front, and he made up his mind to again enter the service of his country, this time as a soldier.

Accordingly the youngster came to Bangor, and, in

company with another Bluehill boy, James Arthur Greene, made his application for enlistment at the recruiting station now being conducted by Mr. McKinley and others in the Adams building on Columbia Street.

The sergeant in charge of the station in the absence of Capt. Frier took the names of the boys, who are the same age. They decided to hang to it and were given lodgings and food pending the arrival of the recruiting officer to swear them in. They passed the examination of Dr. Bryant without trouble.

On Monday, however, Hinckley's father arrived in town from Bluehill and called on his son. He thought his son could do better in Bluehill than in Manila and said so. The parent gave no orders and refused to interpose his objections seriously to his son's enlistment. He only came up to file advice with the young man.

When the news of this reached Capt. Frier, on Monday night, he at once said that he would under no conditions accept Hinckley; he would allow the enlistment of no minor whose parents objected in any way to his going into the army.

Young Hinckley concluded that he would better stay out, and he and his father were at last accounts, at the Hayward, Summer Street, pending their departure for home.

But Gus did enlist in the army on September 29, 1899. Perhaps his father had a change of heart, or possibly the son acted without the knowledge of his father.

On the day of his enlistment Gus began to keep a diary of his service and proudly wrote: "I enlisted in the United States Volunteer Army for service in the Philippines. My friends gave me the devil when they read of it in the *Commercial*."

The young man continued to keep a service journal until the second day after his discharge, March 15, 1901. He used seven separate little books. He included fifteen sketches of the flags of different nations, ten maps of towns and parade grounds, and three plans of forts and churches.

On Monday, October 2, 1899, Hinckley and other volunteers left Bangor. He wrote a lively account of the railroad journey to Vermont:

> Left with five others this afternoon at 1:45 on the "Flying Yankee" (fast train). Spent the night in Portland at the Lincoln Park house. Had two quarts of whiskey on the train and we made sport for the occupants of the smoker. Slept in the great unfurnished chamber in the roof of the L. P. House. Howled and yelled all night.

The Maine boys went to Fort Ethan Allen in Vermont. There they drilled, marched, and had target practice. Hinckley was no sharpshooter: "Spent this hot day at target practice. My score is too rotten to put down on paper." He was in Company G, but his best friend, a young Mr. Thine, was in Company K. Hinckley wrote, "We live rotten in Company G. Miserable food. Thine, my friend in Company K, gives me a good handout every evening."

> Sat. — 11th — Thine and I went to Burlington last night. Bought supply of tobacco, stamps and blank books for diaries. Bought a Fountain pen from one of the boys. Snow this afternoon and our battalion marched over two miles for a skirmish drill and pitched our dog-tents in the snow — almost froze.

Sun. — 12th — Sarg. Fuller, Corp. Laird and I went
to Winnaski and took dinner in a restaurant. Put away
a pile of grub.

The troops went by train to New York City and on
November 15 boarded the United States transport ship
Meade. Hinckley made many comments on the voyage from
New York to Manila: "Had my wool clipped snug to my
head today. I look like a scalped person." "There was a
service on the mess deck, and the way the parson flew
around when an extra wave came was great fun." "I ought
to be thankful on Thanksgiving Day but I am not. I can't
help contrasting it with last Thanksgiving Day dinner that
we took with the Merrill Hinckleys. There was everything
to eat and we had a merry time."

Hinckley made daily comments about the ports of call on
the trip to Manila: Gibraltar, Port Said, Aden in Arabia,
Columbo on the Island of Ceylon, and Singapore on Christmas Day. Likely the young soldier was homesick. He wrote
that the bay reminded him of Penobscot. He spent hours
writing letters and keeping his journal:

> I am resolved to do my whole duty while I am in the
> army, not to shirk any work, no matter how disagree-
> able it is, and get along with all men, non-coms and all.

G Company of the 43rd Regiment went ashore on January 2, 1900, a cloudy day, and had a full day's march to a
camp near Manila where the soldiers were stationed. On
the march from 6 A. M. to 9 P. M. they had only a piece of
hardtack and a slice of bread. The camp was dirty; the
drinking water had to be hauled; white ants and mosquitoes were numerous; and the food was "awfully scarce."

The scarcity of food continued. The hungry soldier wrote, "Had a small slice of bread and pickle for breakfast." "This noon I was so hungry that I was glad to pick up a piece of bacon from the ground."

Hinckley's regiment, the 43rd, lived in two different camps outside Manila. The first task of the soldiers was to clean up the camps. Hinckley's comment was, "The army uses the 43rd as a mop." The regiment's stay near Manila was not without pleasures: trips to the city to see the sights and to feast on salmon, chicken pie, beef pot pie, and ham.

On January 18, the soldiers of the 43rd Regiment embarked on a number of "nasty little boats." G company slept on deck where they were so crowded that they could not unroll their bedding. They were aboard the vessel until the 24th. It rained every night. Hinckley once wrote: "Rained all the afternoon and the awnings are so old that they are worse than none. We can't get below so we have to stay in the wet. This is worse than the Watermost depth of Hell."

The regiment went ashore on the island of Leyto, recently captured from the natives who were in rebellion against the provisional government set up in the Philippines by the United States. Hinckley's company lived in an old schoolhouse. The food was more plentiful.

However, there were vexations. The insurgents made hit-and-run attacks on the town. The soldiers became drunk and fought each other. And there were what Hinckley called "hykes." His first one was on February 25, and he did not find it a pleasurable experience:

Feb. 25 — On our march passed through a number of small villages. The paths were terrible; sank into clay at every step from three inches to two feet. Went up hills almost straight and then down. Crossed the river two or three times, and no end of little brooks. Ten long miles we struggled along, and when we reached our destination, found we were on a Wild Goose Chase.

On March 22, Company G moved to Gondora, a town burned by the rebels. Here they were nearer to the insurgents. There were frequent fights with loss of life on both sides. Hinckley showed no grief for a dead or wounded "nig" or "boloman," names he used for the insurgents. From Gondora he now and then went on "hykes" with the aim of destroying native property.

While stationed at Gondora, Hinckley had time to make maps of the town and vicinity, to visit churches and listen to native music. Once he met a Spaniard who owned a graphaphone that he played for the soldiers. It is evident that Hinckley was learning to respect the religion of the natives and to like their music:

April 8 — The bishop of Cebu is here and said High Mass. Afterward there was a procession. Everyone had palm branches in their hands, and the band played but the bells rang so loudly that I could not tell what they were playing. It was very impressive.

In the summer, an infected foot sent young Hinckley to the hospital where he stayed from July 25 to 31. Statements in his journal show that he enjoyed his stay in the hospital:

July 30 — It is good to have a bed and sheets, pillow slips and mosquito bars.

July 31 — My friend Shaky brings me grub. Have fish, eggs, chicken and bread.

The following month he seemed to have more time to himself. He wrote in his diary sketches about the Filipino natives, their character, houses, food, work, and attitudes. He had time to write numerous letters. He went to the native church and in one church played the organ, rejoicing that he had not forgotten how to play. He studied signaling and was admitted to the Signal Corps. He wrote of seeing millions of grasshoppers whose passing darkened the sun.

In October 27, 1900, Hinckley went aboard an unnamed boat to serve as a headquarters guard. The boat called at several coastal towns and at one of the towns he was among those invited to a concert given at the home of "a Filipino gentleman." At another town they heard about the death of President McKinley. On November 20, they left a town with two schooners in tow. Aboard the boat, Hinckley, the long-time critic of army cooks, became the cook: "I am cook today. Baked some beans today and all were loud in their praise. They were baked all night and until dinner. They were genuine homecooked beans."

By December 3 he was ashore at the headquarters and expressed delight, "This Headquarters Guard is a first rate outfit. Have almost nothing to do but keep clean. Taclaban is the best place I've seen in the islands."

The journal shows that Hinckley needed more than personal cleanliness to keep him happy. He needed to be busy. Soon he was teaching English to a "roomful of Chinese." He had often written of the Chinese in a kind manner and recorded how they had befriended him. On January 15 he started to study tactics and he discussed with a friend the possibility of going to Siam. He welcomed a little excitement: the burglary of the office safe and an earthquake at midnight. On March 13, a day before he received his discharge papers, he saw General Arthur MacArthur, the father of General Douglas MacArthur. Hinckley wrote in his journal:

> General MacArthur reviewed the 35th Infantry last night; afterwards made them a fine speech. He isn't much of an orator, but what he said was good . . . . The General is a very commanding looking man.

In his last days in the service, Hinckley thought about the natives. He wrote of them, "These people are intelligent, good looking, and just as good as Americans. I am ashamed to be fighting for the United States against the liberty of such a people."

He also thought about himself and wrote a poignant estimate of his character:

> I am unfortunate in being cranky, or perhaps a better word is reserved, and make friends very slowly. Anyone I don't like, I can't help letting them know it. And most of those I would like to know don't care a damn about me. So I spend most of my time reading and wandering around alone.

Prior to Hinckley's discharge, he received permission to remain in the Philippines and join the Manila Police Force, a civilian organization. On March 14, 1901, he wrote in his journal, "This ends my soldiering forever I hope."

The last entry in his journal is this:

> Augustus Peters Hinckley
> who is NOT a soldier
> March 15.

But, of course, this was really just the beginning of his adventurous life.

33

Manuel Mello, Newcomer

MANUEL MELLO CAME TO Blue Hill in the mining times of the late nineteenth century. He was an immigrant newcomer and he came alone. I remember him well. In my early childhood he kept a store in the Dunn Block at the Head-of-the-Bay. He was then an old man with bronze face and snow-white hair, and his falcon-like nose and high forehead gave him an aristocratic look. Now and then I went to his store with my Great-uncle, Pearl Parker. My Uncle went to buy cigars and pipe tobacco and to listen to Mr. Mello tell stories. Uncle always bought me a bag of penny candy, and usually the storekeeper gave me a banana which he peeled for me. After Uncle lighted a cigar, he asked Mr. Mello a question that prompted the storekeeper to tell a story. The stories were told in flawless English.

They were in no way as exciting as the stories local tradition told about Mr. Mello. Local tradition, that fabricator of lies and abuser of common sense, was always an active force in old Blue Hill. One of the most exciting stories stated that Manuel Mello came from an old and very rich Portuguese family. He had started his training in a religious order where the boys wore heavy iron collars both day and night. This was too much for young Manuel. He ran away to the South Sea islands where for years he was a beachcomber.

In 1939, Mr. Mello told a Bangor newspaperman how he happened to come to the United States. His account appeared in the December 26 issue of the *Bangor Daily News*. He and his mother and father had lived in the Azores, islands owned by Portugal. His father went to Rio de Janeiro and died there. His mother was evidently well educated. She and her son came to this country in a sailing vessel when Manuel was eleven years old. The boy worked his passage.

As a young man, Manuel went to sea and sailed in all kinds of vessels, schooners, ships, barkentines, and brigs. He was in a number of near-shipwrecks. He told the Bangor reporter of one of his experiences:

> While on the schooner *Kenduskeag* out of Bangor with a load of lumber, a December gale sprang up and blew the masts out of her and carried away two anchors. She nearly went aground on Cape Cod and split herself wide open.
>
> I had signed on as a cook and the night before the big gale, I came on deck and I knew there was a lot of heavy weather making up. Before morning it was howling hell with the sticks out of her. The captain was a Dutchman, and I carried him hot coffee from time to time during the night while he was lashed to the wheel. About six the next morning I looked around and I said to myself

something is wrong, and I heaved the lead. We were in just enough water to float her.

We got a jury rig on her finally and we limped into Salem although there was considerable damage to our load of lumber.

In his later years Mr. Mello left the sea and did a variety of work. At one time he was the ferryman between Bangor and Brewer and took his passengers across the Penobscot in a rowboat. He worked in the Blue Hill copper mines and helped to run the first phone lines to Blue Hill and Bar Harbor. He was likely the first man to install a gas pump in Blue Hill.

Manuel Mello was twenty-four years old when he became a citizen of the United States:

> I can't tell you of the feeling that came over me. I had wanted to be a citizen for a long time. I earned my living here and the government protected me and gave me all the rights and privileges, so I couldn't find one reason why I should not become a citizen. I cherish my citizenship papers and keep them right handy in a cigar box.

Manuel Mello, immigrant, became a good citizen of the United States and a good citizen of Blue Hill.

34

Willis Osgood, Selectman

WILLIS OSGOOD WAS THE FIRST villager whom I knew by name. I met him when I was four years old and beginning to go to church with my father and mother. Going to church was no hardship for me. If I grew sleepy, I stretched out on the cushioned seat and took a nap. If I became restless, Father took me in his lap and fed me Necco wafers.

In my early years of churchgoing, Willis Osgood seemed to me more important than the man up front who did so much talking. Mr. Osgood was a tall man who stood very straight with his head held high. His face, though he must have been fifty, was unlined, his eyes were very blue, and his thick hair was snow white. He was the first man whom we saw on Sunday morning when we went into the entrance vestry. He was pulling the bell rope, often just finishing when we arrived. We lived nearly three miles from the church. In winter and again in mud-time, the journey to church was slow and sometimes perilous.

I saw Mr. Osgood also during the church service because he was one of four men who took up the collection. And he was by far the most handsome — he carried himself as a man of authority. He and his three helpers each carried a polished pole at the end of which was a red velvet bag that dangled a fat red tassel. Dropping my pennies into the red bag was, for me, the climax of the service.

I saw Mr. Osgood a third time when we left church. In fair weather he stood outside the front door and gave each churchgoer a farewell handshake.

In later years I learned that it was Mr. Osgood's sister, Belle Osgood Hinckley, who played the church organ; and that it was his wife, Eva, who was the church treasurer. She always carried a small brown satchel into which she emptied the coins and bills from the collection bags.

Willis Osgood was a descendant of Ezekiel Osgood, Senior, one of the first settlers at the head of the bay. He and his six sons were important men in the village. One of his daughters married Elisha Dodge, and one of his granddaughters married George Stevens. Many of his sons settled between the mountain and the bay and they built beautiful houses, nine of which are standing today. The oldest is occupied by Louise Frederick, a descendant of Ezekiel's son Christopher. Two of the six Osgood brothers, Christopher and David, fought in the Revolution.

When the first meeting house was built on Tenney Hill, Phineas Osgood was one of five men to draw up plans for its completion. The town report put it this way: "They shall present such a plan for finishing the meeting house as shall occur to them." In 1797, when the pews were bid off, Isaac, Phineas, and Daniel each purchased a pew. There were three exits to the meeting house, and Phineas and Daniel

Osgood bought adjoining pews near the front door and
Isaac bought a pew beside the north door.

The Osgoods were great hunters and perhaps they chose
pews as near the outdoors as possible. In summer and fall
when the doors remained open, they may have strained
their ears to hear the bark of a fox. It is a tradition that Daniel
once went hunting in a storm. When he circled back to go
home, he found the tracks of a bear in the snow. In excitement he followed these tracks to his own doorstep. From
Daniel's "bear-tracking" incident came the practice of calling an Osgood son "Cub" or "Bear."

Willis was the great-grandson of Daniel, the miller. But
Willis had no desire to work in the old mill or till the
ancestral acres. He went to Boston and learned the trade of
a meat cutter at Faneuil Hall Market. At the death of his
father, he and his pretty wife, Eva, came back home. He set
up a meat market in a well-lighted basement room. He had
his own slaughterhouse, and he built henhouses where he
raised fowl. He set up "egg routes" run by Eva or his son
"Bear" or a young hired boy. They collected eggs for the
Boston market.

The coming of the summer people brought prosperity to
the Osgood market. The shopkeeper greeted his customers
with great dignity and good humor. They approved of
Willis's starched jacket, his hat made from a paper bag, and
his skill with knife and cleaver. He sold liver and sweet-
breads and hamburg in small cartons that he like to call
"cartoons." Every morning in summer one of the Osgood
helpers drove a delivery cart to Parker Point to take eggs,
steak, chops, and chicken to waiting cooks.

Willis was indeed a busy man, but he was never too busy
to show a helper how to dress a chicken or harness a horse
or wrap a package. He was never too busy to stop to talk

with customers, to loan his bicycle to a neighbor boy, to give a few pennies to a child headed for the candy counter. After work, he helped little "Bear" with his arithmetic. After supper, he walked down the hill to the village store. He wore a suit, a fresh shirt, and a tie. His thick white hair was freshly brushed. His eyes gleamed with the expectation of smoking a cigar with good friends.

Willis Osgood became a selectman. While he was selectman, he had an idea: Blue Hill should have a park. Wilfred Grindle, a farmer whose place was at the edge of the bay, had just died. Mr. Osgood consulted the Widow Grindle, and she consented to sell the field. So Selectman Osgood placed this item in the town warrant: "to see if the town will vote to raise a sum of money to buy Wilfred Grindle's field." The men in town meeting assembled voted a resounding "No." Unkind comments were heard: "Willis must be crazy." "What do we need of a park?" "The idea of spending taxpayers' money for Wilfred's old field!"

Courtesy of Robert Sweetall

The next year the same item appeared; the same negative vote resulted. And so it was year after year. But every year there were a few converts to the idea of a park. Women began to nag their husbands to support the purchase. Mothers began to say, "What a great place for the Sunday school picnics!"

Eventually the men at town meeting voted that the town should buy the Grindle field.

For decades people have been enjoying the park with its view of the bay, Parker Point, and Cadillac Mountain. Townspeople should call Willis Osgood blessed.

35

Emma Jean MacHowell, Librarian

ON THE DESK AT THE BLUE HILL PUBLIC LIBRARY is a brass plaque that bears the name of Emma Jean MacHowell, one of the librarians of the town's Ladies Social Library when the library was in the town hall.

Miss MacHowell was no longer the librarian in the days of my childhood. She was at home tending an ailing mother. But now and then I met her on the street. She was tall and slender. Her step was quick; her greeting, cheerful. She liked to talk with the village children about the books that they were reading. When I attended the grammar school that was located beside her long, rambling home, I often saw her. On the warm days of spring and fall she hung the parrot's cage on the porch. The parrot was not a silent occupant. When the schoolhouse windows were open, we could hear his screams and on rare occasions he spoke a few words, and they were never polite. We children were frightened of old Mother MacHowell, but we liked the daughter. If she was on the porch or in the flower garden, we lingered to talk with her and we were known to ask her help in diagraming a sentence or reviewing a book.

My parents admired Miss MacHowell. Father used to say: "Too bad she did not go to college. She is a very bright woman." Mother said: "It is strange that she never married. She was a very handsome young woman and could have had any man she chose. You recall that Mrs. Howe's stepson, the one who owned a yacht, was crazy about her." Father was unimpressed with the Howe suitor and remarked: "Howe was a snob. She would have done better to marry a local man."

Popular opinion was that Mrs. MacHowell and *her* mother, Mrs. Judah Chase, felt that no one was good enough for Emma Jean. Both Emma Jean's mother and grandmother made much of their family history. Grandma Emma Chase was proud that she was the daughter of Edith Wood and Nehemiah Hinckley. The Woods and Hinckleys were among the town's first settlers. Emma's first marriage was to the son of Dr. Tenney. When Tenney died as a young man, she married Captain Judah Chase, a deep-water sailor. Her twin sons, William and John Tenney, went to Boston and Portland. Two beautiful stained glass windows in the Blue Hill Congregational Church bear witness to their prosperity and generosity. Emma Jean's mother was the only child of Emma's second marriage. Probably both Mrs. Chase and her Tenney sons regretted that the daughter married a man "from away" who came to town to make tin cans for the fish cannery on the town wharf. Mr. MacHowell seemed to have been an unhappy man. He fenced his yard to keep out the children. He retreated to the barn when callers came. He had a violent quarrel with a neighbor over the ownership of a spring. Merrill Hinckley, the keeper of the village store and the owner of a Great Dane, used to remark, "My dog growls at no man with one exception, Mr. MacHowell."

Her father's unfriendliness may have shadowed Emma Jean's childhood. Pinched circumstances shadowed her adulthood. But she seemed to lead a joyous life. Every Saturday afternoon she was at the library and every Sunday she went to church and sat in the Judah Chase pew. Before her mother's health failed, Emma Jean went to Boston and to Portland to visit her uncles, men who gave her generous gifts. She took part in the social life of the little village. She went to concerts and lectures; she belonged to the church circle and the Relief Corps. In winter she played cards; in summer she picnicked. In all seasons she called on her neighbors, Mrs. Partridge and Mrs. Morse, and others.

After her mother's death she went to Portland and kept house for her uncle John Tenney in his old age. She became interested in an orphanage. Perhaps she worked in the orphanage. When she came home to stay, she brought with her a beautiful little orphaned girl. The child had an incurable heart disease, but she grew better under the care of her foster mother. I recall once seeing the two in church. During the sermon the child slept with her head in Emma Jean's lap. During the last hymn Emma Jean remained seated. It was as though she could not bear to awaken the sleeping child.

After the death of the child, Emma Jean lived on in the old house filled with the mementos of the Hinckleys and Tenneys and Chases. When she had callers, she poured tea from the silver pot that Captain Judah Chase had purchased in New York. If the house held unhappy memories, she did not dwell on them. She accepted old age with grace and dignity.

I am not the only person who recalls Miss Emma Jean MacHowell with admiration. In 1930, R. Manly Grindle, the son of the village doctor of the late nineteenth century, published a book of verse about the people of "Clarksville" (most certainly Blue Hill). I quote the lines about the librarian. It seems only fair to write that not all of his verses express admiration for the people of Clarksville.

Jane MacHowell

'Twas Jane MacHowell ran the library in Clarksville. Jane was forty — and had been so for years — unmarried, lived for Ma and Pa and books. Her height and low, soft way of speaking seemed to lend an air of almost regal charm. One wondered why some man — those blue Scotch eyes and Highland hair and slender neck and grace would beautify to captivate; no doubt of that. But Jane was born for books, and books became her forte. She never missed a Saturday between one and five for fifty years, and when report she'd died came out, they flew the flag half-mast and carved her stone: — The debt is paid at last.

36

Otis Littlefield, Doctor

DR. OTIS LITTLEFIELD came often to my home in the days of my childhood. He came twice to take stitches in my tongue, which once was cut by glass, once punctured by a pencil. He saw me through scarlet fever, the measles, and numerous feverish spells. His voice was always comforting; his hands were always cool. When his coat sleeves brushed against my pillow, I could smell the fragrance of hay and medicine. When he left, he spoke reassuring words to my father and mother. At the head of the stairs he turned and said to me, "When I was young, I was very generous. I gave the mumps and the measles to all my friends."

The doctor lived in a large village house between the Thomas Lord and Judge Chase residences. When I went to the house with my aunt, I saw an organ, rich carpeting, and beautiful china. I believed that the doctor was born rich. I was wrong.

He was born in 1861 in West Sedgwick near the Blue Hill line. His mother was Drusilla Gray, the daughter of Asa

Gray. His father, Samuel Littlefield from Penobscot, was a sailor who died of smallpox and was buried at sea. The widowed Drusilla gave her Samuel, aged two, to his paternal grandfather and she left the four-year-old Otis with his Gray grandparents. She then went to Blue Hill to live with her aunt, Mrs. Silverman.

For four or five years little Otis lived happily in the Gray home where there also were two daughters and three sons of Asa Gray. His grandmother Gray kept house much as her mother had. She washed, carded, and spun yarn from the wool of seventy-five sheep; she wove woolen cloth on her great loom and knit stockings for her family. She dried blueberries on the attic floor and gathered lobelia, wormwood, goldthread, snakehead, tansy, thoroughwort, and cherry tree bark to dose her family and the neighbors. His grandfather owned three cows, young cattle, sheep, two yokes of oxen, and three hogs. He raised enough corn to feed his stock. He caught and sold eels and alewives and he cut wood that he took by scow to Castine, where he sold it. In Otis's childhood his grandfather built a new house, one that did not have a fireplace in the kitchen.

When Otis was seven years old, he went to Penobscot to live with his Grandfather Littlefield. He was homesick, and when he started to run back to Gray's Corner, Grandfather Littlefield chased him back with a stick and punished him. Soon his uncle, Stephen Littlefield, took him to Belfast to live in the home of Jerry Littlefield, another uncle. For the first time little Otis saw carpeting. Jerry Littlefield and one daughter were kind to Otis, but the wife and an older daughter nagged him about his country ways and country speech.

The next fall Jerry Littlefield handed on the boy to Oliver Chase, a worker in a Belfast shipyard. Chase and his wife had just lost their only child, a boy of Otis's age. Otis wore the dead boy's clothes, played with his toys, and was called "Otis Chase." He was sent to school where he had caring teachers and learned the joy of memorizing poetry. He had found a home.

But in a year and a half, Mrs. Chase was committed to the insane asylum and Mr. Chase broke up his home. He sent Otis to live with his brother-in-law, who was a hard taskmaster. Otis was overworked and underfed and not allowed to go to the rural school.

His mother rescued him from this unhappy home, and took him to Castine, where she bought him a coat with brass buttons. A relative set them across the Bagaduce River and they walked to Gray's Corner. Otis's aunts and uncles were asleep and the grandparents had just put on their white nightcaps when Otis and his mother got to the Gray home. In an autobiographical sketch, Dr. Littlefield wrote thus of his homecoming: "I was at last home again from a foreign shore. Never so happy in my life."

After two more spells of working out for his board, there was a return to Asa Gray's where he was always happy and well treated. Otis was interested in the doctor who came to see his ailing grandmother. To him he said, "I'm going to be a doctor when I grow up."

After his grandmother died, Otis went to Blue Hill where his mother was still living with Mrs. Silverman. He worked his board in the home of Deacon Joseph Hinckley. There he was well treated and allowed to go to Blue Hill Academy, where the tuition was a dollar and a half for three months. In 1879 the Baptist minister, Mr. Woodbury, suggested that young Littlefield get a teacher's certificate. The minister himself gave the examination and graded Littlefield high on everything except handwriting. Years later the doctor excused himself by writing, "My fingers were covered with pitch from cutting wood."

Otis's last venture in working for his board was in Bucksport where his mother had gone to be the house-keeper for Ivory Grant and his daughter. Otis worked by caring for Grant's ten horses. While he was in Bucksport, he went to Bucksport Seminary.

When he and his mother returned to Blue Hill, the widow Silverman had married Dr. George A. Yeaton, a naval surgeon. At Yeaton's suggestion, Otis went to work in the mines, where the working day was ten hours. In the late summer Yeaton took Otis with him to Swan's Island and suggested that he apply to teach the winter term of school on the island. He applied and was hired. He loved the islanders, his island boarding place, and the island preacher. He was later to write: "Islanders are the best people in the world."

In the fall of 1880 and the winter and spring of 1881, he alternated schoolteaching with mining. He had started to study medicine: "I had bought forty dollars' worth of regular medical books and learned what I could by study-ing bones, livers, animal hearts, and so forth. I did much of this at Swans Island and nights after I did a day's work at the mines."

In his autobiography Dr. Littlefield explained how he earned his medical degree. For nine months of the year he went to the Portland School of Medical Instruction that was over the Canal National Bank on Free Street. It was operated by the doctors of Portland. For three months of each year he went to Bowdoin College in Brunswick where he took courses in medicine. The course required four years of work and study. The passing of a final examination was required, including mastery of Latin.

In June 1881, Littlefield had gone to Portland with sixty-five dollars in his pocket. He paid sixty dollars to the treasurer of the School of Medical Instruction. He went to the Preble House where he told the proprietor that he would wash dishes and scrub floors for his board and room. Montgomery Gibson laughed and said, "You will not have to wash and scrub. You can tend the coatroom." Soon the new employee was sorting the mail, tending the bar, and working in the billiard room. He learned to mix twenty different drinks and to play a good game of billiards. He often played billiards with Herman Kotzmar, the organist for whom Cyrus Curtis named the organ that he gave to the city of Portland.

Kotzmar was not the only famous person whom Littlefield met. He often saw Longfellow resting in the garden of his family home. One day he stepped inside the gate, spoke to him, and told him how much he enjoyed memorizing the lines of the poem *Evangeline* . At Bowdoin he came to know General Joshua Chamberlain, one of the heroes of Gettysburg, who for a time was president of the college.

He found time to visit libraries and museums, to see plays at the Jefferson Theater, and to attend lectures on geology and astronomy, subjects in which he took a lifelong interest. He wrote that he became "a cracker jack" at dissecting. His comments on his years of education in Portland and Brunswick give evidence of both his success and his happiness:

> I was getting a wider number of friends and feeling happier all the time.
> Things went well with me and I stuck to my work.
> I was thankful that I had held on hard with a firm grip and accomplished my purpose.

The four years between 1885 and 1889 were the most exciting of Otis Littlefield's life. Immediately after graduation, he went to Boston where he boarded the steamer *Cumberland*, built at Bath. It ran between St. John and Boston with stops at Eastport and Portland. He was one of the cleaning staff. He wrote that the work was easy, that the workers had as good food as the passengers, that he did not have a minute of seasickness.

At the end of the summer Otis Littlefield went to Gloucester where his mother was living with John McNish, whom she had recently married. He met one of his mother's neighbors, Mary Saunders, "an ideal, sensible young woman." They began to exchange letters and there was soon an understanding that they would marry.

The steward of the *Cumberland* had suggested that Littlefield go to Jacksonville, Florida, for the winter and apply for work at the Webster House, whose proprietor the steward knew. He followed the suggestion and went south, going to Savannah by steamboat and completing his journey by train. After working the winter at the Webster House, he accepted a position in a Wisconsin summer hotel owned by the proprietor of the Webster House.

Soon Littlefield turned from hotel service to more exciting work. He went to Chicago where he worked for the Pinkerton Detective Agency, which advertised its services with the slogan, "We never sleep." The boy from Maine was delighted with the expensive uniform provided for him. His first assignment was at Council Bluffs near Omaha, Nebraska, where he and other agents protected railroad property during a strike. He returned to Chicago where he witnessed mob violence and a factory fire in which many women were burned to death. He went to the theater and saw Edwin Booth act in several Shakespearian plays. He had the fun of being a supernumerary in one of them. Twice he left Chicago to serve as a doctor, first at a copper mine near Lake Superior, and then at a levee-building project in Louisiana.

After he left the levee work, he and a friend, whom he called "Whaley," had a special adventure. Littlefield referred to it as "a pilgrimage:" they took a tour of Arkansas and Missouri. Sometimes they hopped a freight train. More often they walked, cooked on an open fire, and slept on the ground. Evenings they entertained each other. "Whaley" sang and told about life in Kentucky. Littlefield recited poetry and described life in Maine.

His last job with Pinkerton was a stint of guarding Chicago warehouses at night. He had time to visit second-hand bookstores and start collecting books, and to become acquainted with members of the Salvation Army and their work with the poor.

He had saved enough money to buy into service with an Illinois doctor. But a letter from his great-aunt Yeaton summoned him to see his sick mother. She recovered from her illness. Otis, now wishing to stay in the East, became discouraged when he could find no Massachusetts doctor who would take him into partnership, so in the spring he went to Bar Harbor to work for a Mr. Webber, a cousin, who was in the business of moving buildings.

In the summer of 1889 he drove to Blue Hill and called on Dr. Yeaton and his wife. Again Dr. Yeaton influenced his life. "I plan to go to Florida for the winter. Why not come to Blue Hill and take over my practice?"

Yeaton never again practiced medicine in Blue Hill. Littlefield spent the remainder of his life there.

In his memoir, Dr. Littlefield wrote only sixteen pages about his years in Blue Hill. He devoted several pages to kind statements about the doctors who preceded him. He wrote that typhoid was common in Blue Hill in his first years in town. In one day he found three cases, one in North Blue Hill, one in the village, and one on Long Island. He mentioned that he mixed his own medicines. In the late nineties and the first decade of the twentieth century, he often went to Long Island three times a week. Then, as many as two hundred men were working in the island quarries and cutting sheds. Once bad weather kept him there for three days. He slept on a mattress of seabird feathers, ate good island food, and smoked in front of a roaring fire. In the afternoons and evenings, his hostesses, two elderly sisters, sat beside him. They, too, smoked pipes.

In Dr. Littlefield's account, there are two major omissions. He failed to write that he was for years "the Democratic kingpin" in town and a fluent talker at town meeting. In 1929, a Democrat in Washington wrote and asked him to recommend someone to be appointed postmaster. The doctor did an unusual thing. He asked the selectmen to call a town meeting and to summon the voters to choose between the two Democrats who were interested in becoming postmaster. Young Ward Snow was the choice of the Blue Hill voters. He received the appointment.

The doctor also failed to mention his interest in local history. He was one of the founders of the Blue Hill Historical Society, a promoter of the 1908 historical observance, a collector of old papers, and a friend and correspondent of Captain R. G. F. Candage, Blue Hill's family historian.

I went often in my young womanhood to the home of Dr. Littlefield. I did not go for medical needs; I went for historical advice. He said to me: "What you should do, girl, is to read and take notes on the records of the town and the two churches."

37

Lizzie Wood, Country Diarist

WHEN I WAS A CHILD, Mother did not object to the noise
that Cousin Olive and I made. Our chatter when we played
school, our shouting when we played Pitt or Parcheesi left
her serene. But when she wrote in her diary, she asked for
relative quiet. She had a place and a time for writing. The
place was the rocking chair by the end kitchen window,
from which she saw the yard and the garden near at hand
and the sprawling hump of Long Island to the south. The
time was in the early afternoon after she had washed the
dishes, taken off her percale apron, and tied on a white one
ruffled with lace.

In her diary she wrote the weather and the temperature
of the preceding day. She always wrote of Father's activities
and her own. She believed completing a dress, churning
butter, and cleaning a room were worthy of record. Neighborhood news and national catastrophe did not go unre-
corded. She ignored politics but gave due attention to

depressions, wars, and the deaths of presidents. Mother belonged to the Baptist Church, the Grange, the Rebekah Lodge, the Village Improvement Society, the Blue Hill Historical Society, the Garden Club, the Extension Service, and League of Women Voters. All received praise in her diary. The doings of her numerous relatives from Seattle, Washington, to Orland, Maine, were grist for her daily chronicle. Mother's 1903 journal was kept in a notebook designed for keeping accounts. On the back of the front cover she wrote,

> J. F. Wood and Wife
> The Wigwam

"Wigwam" was the name that the young couple playfully applied to the farmhouse where they lived. The record in the book was kept entirely by the wife. But John's name appears frequently:

> John worked at the shed. [The shed
>   where granite was cut.]
> John took Prince to the village to be
>   shod.
> John gather apples.
> John froze ice cream.
> John and I went to Highland Grange
> John and I went to church and had
>   Sunday dinner at Mother's.
> John and I spent the evening with
>   Welland and Nettie.

Mother's 1903 diary gives an outline of a disruption in her family's life. She and my father were living in the old Friend farmhouse. Beside the house was the new barn with a cow and Prince, the black gelding colt. There were hens in the pen, a pig in the sty. There were homegrown vegetables, home-preserved fruits, and home-raised apples in the cellar. She had been looking forward to a happy winter at home, with her father and mother living to the west of her and her brother-in-law, Arthur, and her sister-in-law, Nellie, living to the east. Then came the bad news. I quote from the diary:

> The Chase Granite Company has stopped work and so John is out of a job. He walked to the Grange Store this afternoon and phoned Mr. Pert in New Hampshire that he would come to Redstone next Saturday.

Actually, Father and Mother did not leave home for sixteen days. The diary tells how busy they were disposing of some of their possessions:

> John has sold 3 barrels of potatoes. We'll take a barrel of potatoes and apples with us. He sold the squashes for 2 cents a pound. I sold a rooster and six pullets to Nellie for $3. Mrs Doyle is anxious to buy our Prince but we have decided to keep him. Arthur paid $8 for the pig. He will keep our cow for us until we come home.

It was evident that Mother did not welcome the move to Redstone. She wrote: "I hate to go away, especially on Mother's account."

They left home on October 15, driving to Sedgwick where they boarded the *Frank Jones,* a steamer Portland-bound. Mother's diary gives an account of the October journey. The aunts to whom she referred were her father's sisters. Aunt Fan was a neighbor; Aunt Georgia lived in Massachusetts.

Thursday, October 15.

We had a beautiful day as far as the weather had to do with it. But I hated to start for Redstone. We rode to Sedgwick with Prince. We enjoyed the trip on the *Jones*. Aunt Fan and Aunt Georgia as well as many other Blue Hill people were on the boat. It cost $9.75 for Prince and our old buggy — more than we expected. Prince got along fine. We had a stateroom and got a fair night's sleep.

Friday, October 16. — Portland

Said "Good-bye" to Aunt Fan and Aunt Georgia this morning as they are taking the morning train to Boston. We could not take Prince off the boat until about 9:30 o'clock because the tide was high. While waiting, we got a lunch at the "Dairy Lunch" and paid John's life insurance and bought me a winter coat for $13.98. John harnessed Prince on the wharf and drove to Clarks Stable where he had a good feed. We drove out of the city through the Park about 10:30 o'clock. Prince was not much afraid of the electric cars and we saw only three automobiles.

Drove through Westbrook, Cumberland Mills and Saccarappa, Gorham and West Gorham. The next town was Standish where we stopped to rest Prince and feed him. We ate our dinner in the carriage. After an hour's stop we started for East Baldwin. It was about 4:45 when we got to that village, but we had to push on to West Baldwin. The road was long and through a thick growth of trees. It was dark before we came to a stopping place. We stayed at a public house where we had a good bed, plenty to eat and a good chance for Prince for $2.00.

Saturday, October 17.

We got upon the road again by 7:00. The road to

Hiram was sandy and we encountered much sand from there to Brownsfield. We were afraid that it would rain but we arrived in Redstone just at noon without meeting the storm. Prince did not mind the drive but we feel homesick to-night. I expect that Prince does too.

Mother and Father rented a house and found a barn where Prince stayed and the carriage was stored, but she was homesick. She was lonesome during the nine hours each day Father was at work. She missed her home, her neighbors, and her view of the bay. She found little to do and little to write in her diary. Her daily entry was often "Nothing special, same as usual."

On December 19, the tone of the diary changed. She wrote good news: "John has decided to go home and I am glad."

The journey home was made by train. Father and Prince went ahead of Mother. Father rode with Prince in a boxcar to see that the horse was safe. Mother followed the next day. They met briefly in Bangor. Horse and Father preceded Mother to Ellsworth. When the three were reunited, Prince took his owners to Friend's Corner. I will quote from Mother's journal for a record of the return:

Tuesday, December 22.

Packed our things and hauled them to the Center after dinner. John settled with Mr. Pert; received pay in full to next Thursday ($90). John is going to have a freight car from Conway Center for Prince and our carriage.

Wednesday, December 23.

John and Prince went this morning. I hope they have

not met with any trouble. I have finished packing my trunks; cleaned the house all I could and made a few calls. I shall stay with Mrs. Elliot to-night.

Thursday, December 24.

Caught the first train this morning; had Mrs. Curtis for company as far as Portland. In Portland I bought a few Christmas presents. Bought a pair of shoes for John for $3.50. Bought handkerchiefs, neckties etc. Had a pleasant ride to Bangor — had Mr. Harding for company as far as Waterville.

Found John waiting for me at the station in Bangor. We visited Prince for a while in the freight car, and then went up the street and bought a fur coat for twenty dollars. I wanted to go to Ellsworth with John and Prince in the freight car but could not get permission, so I was obliged to stop at the Penobscot House. We wanted to be together on Christmas Eve.

Bluehill Mt., Bluehill, Maine.

Courtesy of Robert Sweetall

December 25 — Christmas Day

Arose at 4:30 and took the six o'clock train to Ellsworth. John rode with Prince in the box car. It was a beautiful morning. Frost on the ground but no snow. Met my Husband in the station. We took breakfast at the American House. Bought a few little things at the stores. Took Prince from the box car; put the carriage together and started "full sail" for Friend's Corner at a little after ten o'clock. The folks were glad to see us. We built a fire in the Wigwam. Husband and I were some glad to be home and so was Prince.

Mother's diaries (1903–69) show that she found contentment in her home and town and that she never lost her relish for life.

38

Lena Snow, Sunday School Superintendent

Sunday was the happiest day of the week during the years of my childhood. It was the day when we dressed in our best clothes and went to the hilltop church. The message of the sermon seldom reached my immature mind, but I felt the beauty of the service, the friendliness of the congregation, and the loving nearness of Father and Mother. It was the day when we alternated family dinner between our home and Grandmother's, and when the afternoon was spent in storytelling and good talk.

But most important of all to me, Sunday was the day when I went to Sunday school, which was presided over by Mrs. Lena Snow, a village housewife who had fallen heir to the superintendency from her doctor-father, Rufus Grindles. Once the church service was over and our parents and elders had left for the chapel or home, Mrs. Snow took charge.

242

She marched to the small desk in front of the pulpit. She carried such a basket as Little Red Riding Hood had when she went to visit her grandmother. She had a collection of belongings which we children watched her unpack. There were her quarterlies, her tap bell, the attendance cards, a dust cloth, a box of cough drops (a precaution taken lest the session be disturbed by hacking children), and a jar of hard candies which were meant for the little children only, and in the basket there was always what we children called "the decoration." It might be a plant or a shell or a fan or a bit of coral from the Snow parlor whatnot. Now and then, she brought for her desk a marble vase in the form of a hand.

Brisk tapping to the hand bell brought the school to order with each class in its appointed spot: the little folks to Mrs. Snow's right and the big boys and girls in the back of the church. The session was opened by the singing of a hymn. Then we repeated the "Golden Text" of the previous Sunday, a Bible verse printed on a little colored picture card which had been given to each of us.

After Mrs. Snow had read the Scripture, she prayed. And as my mother said, "Mrs Snow was a master hand at praying." She prayed with earnestness, with sincerity, and with the certainty that her prayers would be answered.

Her petitions always had the flavor of an almanac because she never failed to mention the sweetness of June days, the flare of turning maple leaves, the frost rime in the fields, or the whiteness of January drifts. Nor did she forget the blessings of the preceding week: a new baby in the minister's family, a chimney fire safely extinguished, the presentation of a school play were all included in her chronicle of thanksgiving. She also looked forward to the coming week and asked strength for its tasks, which she took care to list. The conclusion of her prayer was always the same, and it was a conclusion in which we children were expected to join. When she softly gave the signal, "Now children," we repeated with her, "and never let us forget that God is love. Amen and amen.

Once the opening exercises were over, each class turned to its lesson and Mrs. Snow momentarily relinquished the helm of activities to Miss Julia Saunders, a cheerful wisp of a woman who played the piano and served as Sunday school secretary. She passed the envelopes into which we dropped our class collection of pennies, and she distributed to the older children Sunday school papers whose front-page stories and back-page puzzles often drew our attention from the discussion of the lesson.

During the lesson period, Mrs. Snow moved from class to class and, as she had studied the lesson of each, she was in a position to throw in a comment or ask a pertinent question. Her patrol of the church was disciplinary as well as instructional. A noisy child might find himself in isolation in a back pew where he could review with regret the passing of a note or a scuffle with a seatmate. On rare occasions, a young culprit was taken into the church vestibule where he was administered a spanking.

By the time the school was ready to close, the door would have been opened to let in Rex, the huge white and tan dog of the Snow family. Rex, with a sigh of pleasure, always settled himself under a marble-top table by the bookcase. The dog was a favorite with the pupils, though our elders felt that his presence was out of place in a church, an observation never whispered to his owner. But Rex was always on his good behavior, so he well deserved the sobriquet of "Sunday School Dog," a name we children gave him.

It was at the Christmas concert that our kindly superintendent was at her best. She honored the occasion by putting on her best wool dress with a tatting collar and a cameo. We knew that she shared our excitement and anticipation as she helped our teachers group us into close formation in the front pews. The remainder of the pews were occupied by our parents and friends who had come to hear us recite our "pieces" and to watch Santa and his helpers pick the tree.

The concert started like a usual Sunday school session with Mrs. Snow's long prayer. A special collection was taken for the orphanage in Alaska, a charity that had been dear to her father. In her offertory prayer, she never failed to mention her father and to thank God that the children of her Sunday school had homes and parents.

The pieces and the presentation of a few tableaux was a long process always complicated by a few children forgetting their lines or refusing to go onto the stage. Mrs. Snow, from long experience, knew how to deal with both problems. In an unfluttered tone she would say, "Roger does not feel like saying his piece just now. When he feels like speaking, he may raise his hand and we'll be glad to hear him then."

Invariably, Roger's hand was later raised and he recited his piece with success. She gave a faltering performer so much confidence that the child was able to go on.

When the concert was over, we awaited with excitement the coming of Santa, whose arrival was signaled by the sharp sound of sleigh bells. We never saw Santa's reindeer but we never doubted that they were outside the church. It seemed fitting that Mrs. Snow should greet Santa with a friendly handshake and name the big boys and girls who would help in giving out the gifts.

Every child was given a candy bag made of white netting

and marked with a bit of rough paper on which was written his or her name. The bags had been made, filled, and marked by Mrs. Snow and her assistants. Each teacher gave her pupils pencils or bookmarks or some other small tokens. Usually a parent placed a gift on the tree for his child. The tree itself was for children, but our parents took pains to remember the teachers, the minister, and Mrs. Snow. Santa always saved the gifts for the grown-ups to the last, and when he gave Mrs. Snow her present, to the delight of the pupils he placed a kiss on her flushed cheek. We felt that if anyone ever deserved a kiss from Santa, our Sunday school supervisor did. I have never forgotten Mrs. Snow and her friendliness, her dignity, and her sincerity. In my adult years, I have never forgotten her often-repeated dictum: "God is love."

39

The Piper Family

By 1929 SAILBOATS AND STEAMBOATS no longer connected
Blue Hill to Rockland and Boston. Because the sardine
factory had burned, tramp steamers no longer came into the
South Blue Hill harbor. Automobiles and trucks linked Blue
Hill to Ellsworth and Bangor.

Piper's Express was symbolic of the transportation revolution that overtook Blue Hill in the 1920s and 1930s. People
in Blue Hill village came to tell time by the departure and
arrival of Piper's Express trucks to and from Ellsworth.
Four times a day, six days a week, the trucks met the Maine
Central trains at nine, ten, four, and six.

Mr. Minot Piper, his wife and five sons, had moved to the
Head-of-the-Bay in 1911 and occupied a house on the Mill
Brook before moving to Grindleville, a neighborhood outside the village. Mr. Piper, a painter of signs, sleighs, and
carriages, did business in a building owned by James Bettell
on the town wharf.

247

In 1920 the family moved back to the village and bought the three-story Pendleton House, erected years before by Jonah Holt. The Piper family lived on the lower floor and rented the upper floors. One room became the freight office for Piper's Express. Minot Piper tore down the old livery stable and built a garage. In the garage he installed a repair shop and a forge.

In 1918 Minot Piper and his son Cyrus started a freight business, and later the other sons, Luther, Arthur, and Clifford, joined the business either as part-owners or employees.

Cyrus Piper told me about his years of collecting the mail at the Ellsworth station. When the mail bags were thrown from the mail car to the station, he picked up the pouches for Blue Hill, Sedgwick, Brooklin, Brooksville, Penobscot, Deer Isle, and Stonington, and took them to the Ellsworth post office, where the mail was sorted for each town. He then took the pouches to the Blue Hill office, where another man picked up the mail for the surrounding towns.

Cyrus Piper recalled long years of driving over dirt roads. In the spring the roads were muddy; in the summer they were dusty and "washboardy"; in winter, snow-covered and icy. The Piper brothers plowed the road to Ellsworth using their trucks and home-forged plows. Before the state assumed the care of snow removal, the town of Surry paid the Pipers six hundred dollars each season. The state later hired the Pipers to do the job of removing the snow between Blue Hill and Ellsworth.

Cyrus Piper had high praise for the Rio trucks that he drove. They were tough and dependable and used little gas. He could not recall the price of a truck but he did remember that for years gas was thirty cents a gallon; oil, thirty cents a quart; and the price of state registration was twenty dollars for a truck hauling goods for others.

In decades of driving the mail, freight trucks, and passenger vehicles, Mr. Piper had only one accident. One day when he was driving a truck loaded with grain up the steep incline of Morse's Hill, the clutch broke. He was unable to control his vehicle but he did manage to ditch it. In the process, the truck rolled over, he was thrown from the vehicle, and the engine caught fire. Mr. George Morse, standing in his dooryard, saw the accident, ran to the car, and put out the fire.

For many years the Pipers operated both an Ellsworth and a Bangor freight service. In 1918 they brought to town the equipment of the American Smelting and Refining Company of New Jersey. They brought in produce for local grocery stores and the hospital. The freighting for the hospital was done without charge. In early summer and late fall they did a great business hauling trunks for the summer people. One summer the Pipers brought trunks for the Haskell family and for eighteen people who came as "help."

After a few years the Pipers added passenger service to the freight business. A second and third seat were installed in a truck. A fourth seat was added when the brothers took Lodge members on evening jaunts to visit a nearby lodge.

Edward Pemberton drove for the Pipers for thirty-three years and never had an accident. He drove on the Ellsworth route, conveying mail, freight, and passengers. He did errands for people. His most responsible errand was depositing money in the bank for Merrill and Hinckley of Blue Hill and Kane's store of Surry. He assured people that he had no fear of robbery, but he was concerned about the icy roads. Then, there was no sanding of highways. He always enjoyed his passengers, though some of them did things that were a bit strange. He always smiled about a woman on the route who went to Ellsworth several times nearly every day. She went to Ellsworth on his first trip and came home at noontime. She returned to Ellsworth on his afternoon trip and came home with him on his last trip back. Both times she came home with bags filled with groceries. Mr. Pemberton concluded that her husband had both a big appetite and a big paycheck.

Dorothy Piper Duffy, Minot's daughter, told me that it was fun for her to have her father and brothers in the freight and passenger service. On Saturdays she was allowed to ride to Ellsworth and take a friend with her. She recalls that her mother played an important part in the family business. It was Mrs. Piper who in winter warmed the four footstones with which each truck was provided. It was she who provided a meal when husband or son or employee came in hungry. Her mother was very much a short-order cook. The coffeepot and the teapot were always on the stove, and a stew or chowder was at hand for quick heating. There were steak for frying and cooked potatoes for browning.

Changing times forced the Pipers to give up first the passenger and then the freight service. When nearly every family owned a car, there was no need for public transportation. When wholesale companies delivered goods and produce, there was no need for freight service. In 1954 the Pipers went out of the freight business. The Pipers had been in business for three generations and had made the name Piper synonymous with cheerful, efficient service.

40

Mary Ellen Chase, Author

MARY ELLEN CHASE, NOVELIST, biographer, and Bible scholar, lived in two centuries. She was a child of the nineteenth century, a woman of the twentieth.

Her ancestral families, the Chases, the Hinckleys, the Kimballs, the Wescotts, the Lords, the Osgoods, and the Woods were among the first settlers in the land east of the Penobscot River. Her paternal grandmother knew Parson Fisher and had been in the choir at the parson's funeral. In her childhood Mary knew men and women who remembered the War of 1812. Daily she saw men who had fought in the Civil War. It is likely she saw the immigrant soldier James Bettell frequently. He loved to drill the little boys, who were equipped with discarded broomsticks. She knew sea captains who had sailed around the Horn, taken lumber and "ventures" to the Caribbean, and brought back molasses and sugar to Portland. She heard her grandmother tell how her grandfather, Meletiah Chase, had been the lone survivor of shipwreck off the Irish coast; how her grandmother herself had on her wedding voyage been rescued from a sinking ship.

Mary Chase grew up in a village of white clapboard houses whose many-paned windows faced the sea with the Mount Desert hills in the distance. She lived in a house designed by the architect Thomas Lord. Almost next door was the beautiful house that Lord built for his own family. She heard the ringing of bells: the bell of Blue Hill Academy and of the two churches. She walked to the nearby village center that had grown up where the Mill Stream meets the head of the bay. On this margin of the bay there were a dozen or more stores — a millinery shop, a blacksmith shop, and a shoe shop among them. There were three inns where "drummers" put up for the night and rusticators boarded by the week.

Mary Chase's father was the village lawyer and politician who in later years went to the legislature and served on the governor's council. College-educated, he read Greek and Latin. He was a firm father and he expected his children to say "Yes, sir" when they answered his questions or complied with his requests. Her mother, Mabel Lord, had a gentler nature. The Chase children had more advantages than most village children. Their father had a library filled with books. There was a hired girl in the kitchen. Their mother had more time to read to them and help them with their lessons. In the barn were a pony and a matched pair of horses for a Sunday drive. Trips to Ellsworth and Bangor were not unusual.

The Chase family was large. One could say that there were two families: four older children — Mildred, Mary, Edith, and Everett; and four younger children — Olive, John, Virginia, and Newton. All eight became able adults. Mildred was a much-loved secondary-school teacher; Mary became nationally famous; Edith transcribed Jonathan Fisher's journal; Everett was a Portland lawyer; Olive was a Latin teacher; John was a successful businessman; Virginia became a college teacher and a writer of novels and essays; and Newton became head of the Thatcher School in California and a well-known California educator.

Mary Chase's *The White Gate* (W. W. Norton, 1954) and *A Goodly Heritage* (Henry Holt and Company, 1932) tell what it was like to grow up in a country village at the end of nineteenth century. In the first book she tells how her world behind the white gate was enlarged by calls on her neighbors next door and by visits to a house across the village where lived "Do," their mother's stepsister, and her delightfully indolent husband, "Uncle Hen." In *A Goodly Heritage* she makes it clear that the Chase children "grew up under a waning but vigorous Puritanism." There was a clear-cut line between good and evil, right and wrong. There were words that little girls did not use. There were

Courtesy of Robert Sweetall   *Home of Mary Ellen Chase   Bluehill, Maine*

matters about which little girls were supposed to know nothing. The Chase children grew up in a town that was white, Protestant, and Anglo-Saxon. It was an adventure when the children saw a band of gypsies, or met an Indian gathering sweetgrass, or spoke to an Armenian peddler with a heavy backpack.

Writing in the epilogue of *A Goodly Heritage,* Miss Chase rejoiced that she was brought up in "relative simplicity" and had an education based on the classics. She was grateful for the country quiet of her home and "the birthright of long hours of reading."

She became a teacher. *A Goodly Heritage* tells how she happened to become one. *A Goodly Fellowship,* (Macmillan, 1939) describes her career from 1906 to 1939; from rural school to college campus. She interrupted her education at the University of Maine to teach a term at South Brooksville and a year at West Brooksville. It was her father's belief that "if you had anything in you at all, three terms of teaching in a country school would bring it out. If you had nothing, the entrance to college or the return to college then was obviously a waste of both money and time." In her account of her Brooksville teaching she praised country children and the Tapleys who boarded the teachers. She also stated two views that she never relinquished: The personality of the teacher is more important than her intellectual attainments. If the teacher has no enthusiasm for teaching and for subject matter, her students will learn little.

When she returned to Orono, she continued teaching part-time. After her graduation, she taught in the Hillside Home School in Spring Green, Wisconsin. There she was both teacher and housemother. The two sisters who owned the school taught her much about living and teaching. She wrote of her stay, "I entered into many goodly kingdoms of the mind." A desire to study at the University of Chicago led her to leave Wisconsin and take a position at Miss Moffett's School, where the stress was on duty. Miss Moffett encouraged her young teacher to go to Germany for the summer to improve her German. When Mary returned, she developed lung trouble, perhaps from the bad air of Chicago, perhaps from too much concern for duty.

In 1914, doctors sent Miss Chase to Bozeman, Montana, for her health. Two years spent on a ranch restored her and gave her time to write her first book, *The Girl fom the Big Horn Country* (Page, 1917).

After her return to health, she taught briefly in Montana and then entered the University of Minnesota, where she earned her doctorate. She taught at the University of Minnesota and then at the College of St. Catherine. In 1926 she went to Smith College. There she came under the influence of President William A. Nielson. For her, Smith was a "new Jerusalem" where she enjoyed many years of writing and teaching.

In her early years at Smith, she lectured, traveling thousands of miles by train on her lecture trips. She loved seeing the country. She spoke at college graduations and conventions. I once heard her address the Maine Teachers Association at its state convention. She loudly declared: "Your methods of teaching reading may be better than those used thirty years ago, but the readers are filled with material not worth reading."

To write of Mary Chase as a writer is to think of Sarah Orne Jewett, a Maine writer whom Miss Chase greatly admired, just as Willa Cather greatly admired Mary Chase. Mary wrote thirty-nine books. A few, such as *Donald McKay and the Clipper Ships,* are historical. A few, such as *The Writing of Informal Essays,* are educational. Some, such as

Dolly Moses and the Clam Chowder, are for children. She wrote two biographies, *Abby Aldrich Rockefeller,* (Macmillan, 1950), and *Jonathan Fisher, Maine Parson 1768-1847* (Macmillan, 1948). She learned Hebrew so that she could teach and write about the Bible. Her books about the Bible, the Psalms, the prophets, and life in Bible times make delightful reading.

Mary Ellen Chase was best known for her novels. Just as Willa Cather's "feet knew the paths at the old Nebraska farm," so did this Maine writer's feet know the rotten wharfs and shipways where once Maine ships had been built and from which they sailed to faraway lands. *Mary Peters* (Macmillan, 1934) and *David Crockett* (Macmillan, 1935) have the same theme: the decay of maritime Maine.

Probably *Mary Peters* was the most admired of her nine or ten novels. I quote from a review written by Edward Weeks, who was the editor of the *Atlantic Monthly* and a leading literary critic:

> That reflective writer Mary Ellen Chase is seeking to evoke the New England of tradition, the tradition of a coastal people who, men and women, both, went to sea and who there acquired a philosophy and re-sourcefulness which never deserted them though they might retire to upland farms or drowsy villages.
>
> No one writing today is better able to describe Maine's fine and ancient heritage. . . . Her pictures of a Maine farmyard, of the moon at flood tide, an early morning on the uplands, and the fierce exuberance of winter are unforgettable. These passages, in their amassing of detail, in their mood of reflection, fill page after page; they build up a background whose authenticity and loveliness are truly remarkable.

Now and then Miss Chase's novels include a bit of philosophy. I quote the words of Mary Peters: "Life is waiting . . . in order that things to come might find one free and unafraid."

41

William Hinckley, Historian

"ANCESTRAL FRIEND" WAS THE NAME William Hinckley gave me. He liked to remind me that his great-great-grandmother, the widow Polly Kimball, sold her saltwater farm to my great-grandfather, John Friend; that Mrs. Kimball continued to live in the farmhouse and use food and firewood provided by the new owner. I did some reminding of my own. I liked to remind him that I went to school to his mother, Mildred Chase Hinckley; that I wrote "Dear Teacher" letters to her after she was no longer my teacher; that his father, Wallace Hinckley, did over the old farmhouse into which my parents moved in 1907.

But our conversation was not entirely reminders. We wondered where the eighteenth-century town cemetery was located; who built the symmetrically placed piles of stone near the Salt Pond; why a brook was given the strange name of Motherbush. We discussed the settlement of the town, the decline of seafaring, the changes brought by the coming of the summer people. We praised Blue Hillers of the 1860s for their fierce loyalty to the Union.

When we talked about the history of our town and lineage of its families, I deferred to his knowledge. He was Blue Hill's historian.

William Hinckley was a descendant of Joseph Wood, who, with John Roundy, was the town's first settler. He was a descendant of John Peters, the surveyor, who brought the incorporation papers of Blue Hill Academy from Boston to Blue Hill. His great-grandfather, Meletiah Chase, was a sea captain and a village merchant. His Grandfather Chase was a lawyer and judge. His Grandfather Eugene Hinckley was a promoter of the granite industry. Wallace Hinckley, his father, was a promising architect who died as a young man. William was always fascinated by the life of his uncle, Augustus Hinckley.

When William was a little boy, he stayed away from the first grade for several weeks. He already knew his letters and he found the teacher's letter-cards and cut-out books boring. Without his mother's knowledge he spent the mornings and afternoons at the village blacksmith shop. He looked at the coals burning in the forge; he listened to the beat of the hammer against the anvil; he watched the smith fashion tools from iron. He was filled with wonder. At the smithy he caught the habit of listening, watching, and learning.

While still a child, he and his cousin Jerry Hinckley collected bottles that they found in the walls and cellar of the Blue Hill House barn. He once made a plan of the Old Cemetery, recording the names and dates engraved on each stone. He caught an enthusiasm for research and record-keeping. Once he heard his Aunt Mary Ellen say, "Someone ought to keep a record of the Chase Family." William went to Merrill and Hinckley's store and bought a notebook and became the Chase genealogist.

The child William found adventure in his country town. When he was very small, his mother took him on walks to look for birds and flowers. She and he rowed around the inner bay and visited Sand Island. He and Newton Chase tramped the Mill Brook and explored the wood roads. One day when the boys were given two dollars and were told to go for the laundry, they took destiny in their own hands. They used the money to pay for a brief airplane ride above the blue waters of the bay. They went home, confessed, were forgiven, and were sent again on the Tuesday errand.

William knew that a tradition of teaching ran in his mother's family. His mother, Mildred Chase Hinckley, taught at Stevens Academy and at Oak Grove in Vassalboro. His Aunt Mary Ellen was a college professor, and his Aunt Olive was a high-school English teacher. His Uncle Newton was to become a teacher in California. In his own home and his Grandmother Chase's home there were many books. He was encouraged to read, write letters, and take part in adult conversation.

An important part of William's education was village education. He listened to Adelaide Pearson's stories of her world travels. He heard Dr. Littlefield talk about collecting town records. His calls at Max's store, "Wash" Partridge's drugstore, George Mason's quick lunch, and "Sherm" Hinckley's ice-cream parlor broadened his horizons. At "George's" and "Sherm's" he acquired a taste for pie and ice cream. He liked to be at the post office in the summertime and watch the summer people congregate. He walked to the deserted parsonage of Jonathan Fisher and through cracked windows looked at faded rugs covered with papers and books. He biked beyond the village to visit water-filled mine pits, abandoned granite quarries, and wharfs of gray grout.

Everywhere that William went he heard talk about the past: about shipbuilding days, about the mining craze, about the granite boom. He remembered facts and names and became curious to know more about the past.

William's education at Moses Brown prep school and the University of Maine sharpened his interest in nature, science, and history. His working years as a chemical engineer were spent at a paper plant and in Augusta where for twenty-seven years he worked for the state in the field of environmental protection. He traveled over the state of Maine, making many friends as he worked for the protection of Maine's rivers, lakes, and bays. He and his wife, Trudy, lived in the Bangor area where they raised a son, worked in scouting, collected minerals, and became authorities on Maine birds.

Looking Down Main Street, Bluehill, Maine.

Courtesy of Robert Sweetall

When the Hinckleys returned to Blue Hill in 1963, William became the town historian. He and Trudy helped to acquire the Holt house for the Blue Hill Historical Society and were active in furnishing it. As the president of the Fisher Memorial, he showed a versatility worthy of Fisher himself. He set out trees on the property; he built cardholders; he made bibliographies; he wrote scholarly papers; he made maps; and he conducted meetings. He became acquainted with museum directors and scholars.

William became a teaching historian. He researched local history and families. Through his articles in *The Packet*, now published in a book, he shared his findings with others. University history majors sought his advice. He guided children who wrote papers about their homes or village industries and he began a history of Blue Hill. When strangers came to town in search of information, they were told, "Go and ask William Hinckley."

Bluehill, Maine   400,759

Courtesy of Robert Sweetall

42

Roland Howard, Antiquarian

ROLAND HOWARD WAS A LEADING CITIZEN of Blue Hill. He was active in the church, the library, and the Odd Fellows Lodge. He supported the Blue Hill Historical Society, the Fisher Memorial, and the Wilson Museum of Castine. He was the rescuer, restorer, and preserver of town records. When a man was in doubt about the date of a local happening, the value of an antique, or the age of a local landmark, Roland Howard could give him the answer. He was a recognized authority on old houses, furniture, china, glass, and books. He was a collector of antiques, books, and "early Maine imprints."

Roland Howard was born in 1900, the son of Arthur and Annie Horton Howard. Their home was midway up Greene's Hill and had a view of both the mountain and the bay.

In Roland's childhood he saw beautiful things. He saw the bouquets that his mother placed on the kitchen table — wild roses in June, daisies and buttercups in midsummer.

He saw his mother's choice china stored in the long cupboard under the front stairs. On the top shelf was the tea set
that his great-grandparents, Thomas and Sophia Hargrave,
had brought from England. He saw the fancy writing that
his father did. His father's writing tools, paper, and samples
of his writing were kept in a drawer of the sideboard. He
often heard his father say, "Now you children keep your
fingers out of that drawer." Sometimes after a meal his
father took a clean knife or fork and entertained the children
by making imprints of letters on the tablecloth. Years later
Arthur Howard took a ship model to the Blue Hill fair. It
was seen and admired. Soon people from the Mount Desert
summer colony were coming to buy models from Mr.
Howard. Among the purchasers was the editor Joseph
Pulitzer.

Roland saw beautiful things when he crossed the road to
his grandfather's home. In the house he saw an old berry
set, a ladderback chair, and an old rocker cherished by his
grandmother Howard, who prided herself on being a descendant of Elder Brewster of the *Mayflower*. She talked to
Roland about his forebears. In Merrill Howard's cutting
shed he saw gravestones and granite figures of soldiers cut
to memorialize the heroes of the Civil War. Roland marveled at the great windmill that gave power for the tools. He
noticed the order and precision with which his grandfather
stored his tools.

His grandmother, Mary Hargrave Horton, gave him his
first antique, a banded-ware mug. The first antique that he
purchased was a Tobey jug bought from Carrie York, who
lived at the foot of the Sand Hill. He kept the mug and the
jug to the end of his days. Likely the possession of the two
objects prompted him, when he was thirteen, to buy *The
Lure of the Antique*, which cost eight dollars. His brother and
sisters felt that he had wasted his money.

When Roland was thirteen or fourteen years old, he saw the beautiful china and furniture owned by Blue Hill families whose ancestors had made money from shipbuilding or seafaring. Arthur Howard could not cut granite in winter because the yards shut down, so he turned to digging clams. He "shocked" the clams and packed them in glass Mason jars. His sons peddled the clams from door to door. Each boy had a "clam route." As a man, Roland used to remark, "If I got into the kitchen, I always saw the whole house, upstairs and down." No doubt lonesome widows delighted to show off their chests and highboys, their china and their glass.

His horizon broadened when he worked one summer in the James Bettell boardinghouse. One winter he worked for Twining's store delivering groceries using a horse and wagon. He likely took groceries to the Parson Fisher house, where lived the Parson's grandchildren, Augusta and Frederick. It is possible that he was invited into the house to see the Fisher paintings and books.

In 1916 and 1917, Roland worked for the Hyde Windlass Company in Bath where his father and older brother Maurice also were employed . When he bought a bicycle, he began to visit shops and stores and to buy small objects, dishes, candlesticks, and tools. In 1919 he joined the United States Navy, went for his training to Newport, Rhode Island, and became an electrician. He saw service on the *Breckinridge* and *Preston*, ships which visited numerous South American ports. He started to collect maps, programs, tickets, and letters. When he returned home, he added them to his collection of postcards and grade cards.

After he left the navy in 1922, he worked briefly in Boston and then came home to Blue Hill and became a house painter. For thirteen summers he went to Seal Harbor to paint. He spent his winters in Blue Hill, where he worked on his own house and did interior painting for his friends and neighbors.

In 1941 he took a position with the Fore River Bethlehem Steel Company. The next four years were likely the most educational of his life. On Saturdays and holidays he visited historic houses and museums in the Boston area. He went to bookstores, especially to Goodspeed's, a dealer in old books. He went often to the antique departments at Filene's and Jordan Marsh's. When there was a sale, he was there.

In the mid-1930s he had bought the Jerry Faulkner house, built in 1824. In a 1935 diary he made this entry:

Jerry Faulkner House
Jan.1, 1937 — At home in Bluehill working every day in the house on various repairs.

In the diary he reported year after year the work done on the house: a wall torn out, a new staircase built, a new door-rock set, the old porch removed, a chimney rebuilt, a bathroom installed, a furnace set in place. He did the painting and papering and often built bookcases and cupboards.

During the Second World War Roland worked as an electrician in the Fall River Shipyard. When the war ended, he returned home. He wrote in the little diary, "Came home today and shall stay home for good."

Roland was proud of his home. His backyard's beach was washed by the tide. His back windows gave a view of Blue Hill Bay, with Sand Island and Parker Point in the foreground. In the backyard he started a garden. He took the most interest in his spring bulbs. Every year he wrote in his diary the date when the scilla flowered. He also wrote in his diary the date when the ice broke up and left the bay.

In 1945 he opened an antique shop in a little building,

once his brother's blacksmith shop. He went to auctions in nearby towns. His diary shows that he had various ways of acquiring old things:

Bought at Hospital benefit sale five Indian baskets
    for $5.
Made purchases at Copley Plaza Antique Show.
Bought box of relics from Alice Holt.
Painted for Josie Sweet and she paid me with old
    china.

He continued to buy items from Filene's and Jordan Marsh's. In the back of the diary there is a list of twenty-two snuff bottles. Opposite the descriptions are two figures, one is under an M; the other is under a P. I conclude that the M stands for "marked" and the P stands for "paid." He usually paid five dollars or seven dollars fifty cents for bottles marked thirty-five dollars or twenty-five dollars.

He often spoke of one of his first purchases. He bought George Stevens's clock for fifty dollars. In a few years he sold it for two hundred dollars. The sale convinced his brother Maurice that there "was something to be made in buying antiques." His mother's comment on the sale was, "You'll be sorry you ever sold it." And he was sorry. He once said to me, "I bitterly regret that I ever made that sale."

His niece Gay once asked him, "What do you most enjoy collecting?" His prompt reply was, "China and books." He prided himself on his collection of books by Maine authors. Many of these were first editions. His collection included sermons published in the late eighteenth and early nineteenth centuries. After his death his collection of books and papers was sold for one hundred thousand dollars. He collected examples of penmanship made with calligraphic pen strokes. His collection of calligraphy honored his father.

Roland Howard's widowed mother lived with him in the old Faulkner house. Usually the three children of Roland's sister Elizabeth spent their summers with their grandmother and uncle. One of the nephews, long since grown to manhood, made this comment on their summers in the Faulkner house: "Uncle Roland treated us like adults. But he made it clear that we were expected not to touch the wallpaper or the woodwork. He told us 'to look with our eyes' and not to pick up valuable china or glass. He expected us to do our chores well and to do them on time."

His niece Gay recalls the formality of her uncle's manners and his insistence that his nephews and nieces be polite and courteous. But he now and then repeated poetry for the amusement of the children. Sometimes he tried his hand at writing verse. He often quoted to his nieces and nephews Disraeli's comments on Gladstone: "A sophistical rhetorician, inebriated with the exuberance of his own imagination that can at all times command an interminable and inconsistent series of arguments to malign an opponent and glorify himself."

Roland's nieces and nephews regarded their uncle as someone very special. They knew that under his reserve there was a very warm person. His niece Gay wrote, "Everyone ought to have an Uncle Roland. He gave me a very valuable gift — one that I can always have — an interest in family history."

As much as Roland Howard loved his home, he often traveled. He went to Virginia and then to California to visit his nephew David. He went to Cape Cod to visit his sister Elizabeth. He went to visit all his sisters and brothers. He spent long periods of time in New York with his niece Gay.

Everywhere he went, he visited bookstores and museums and historic houses. He never ceased to learn and to collect.

In the years of good health, he was a helpful neighbor. He repaired clocks and recaned chairs for Allie Osgood, a retired teacher. She made pies for him. He cleaned Josie Barker's chimneys and mended her scrapbooks. She patched jackets for him. When he was old, he gave his 1928 Ford to his nephew David. The car had been driven over 100,000 miles. David took it to South Dakota by trailer. Roland walked to the grocery store with an empty white canvas bag. He returned with it filled with groceries. He carried the same bag on his daily trips to the post office and his biweekly trips to the library.

Roland Howard in his old age loved to show his home and his possessions to callers and he made it clear that none of his treasures was for sale. In his old age he took comfort in knowing that some of his belongings had been sold to the Farnsworth Museum in Rockland and that other belongings would be owned some day by the Wilson Museum in Castine, the Blue Hill Historical Society, and the Blue Hill Public Library.

Collectors of antiques, old books, and memorabilia called Roland Howard an antiquarian. He called himself "a self-educated collector with discriminating taste."

43

The Out-Goers

IN EVERY DECADE people have left Maine towns. Some of the out-goers from Blue Hill were pushed to leave. Good farmland became scarce; the soil wore out; the price of timber, wool, hides, and beef dropped. Shipping and shipbuilding declined; shipyards and copper mines, quarries and granite yards closed. Work at the porgy plant, the sardine factory, and the mineral springs was short-lived. Sometimes a personal reason pushed a man to leave town: a broken love affair, a quarrel in the family, a brush with the law, a reputation for being a deserter in the Civil War. Some of the out-goers were pulled away: by the adventure of going to sea, the rich farmlands of the West, the gold of California, and the excitement of the cities.

John Randall was one of Blue Hill's first out-goers. Buying the rights of one of the original proprietors, he came to New Andover in 1768. He was assigned Lot Number 29 and built a house near the Mill Stream, where the present Odd

Fellows building stands. His neighbors were Nathan Parker to the west, Ezekiel Osgood to the east, and Christopher Osgood and John Horton to the north. He and two others built a sawmill on the Mill Stream. Perhaps he left town to fight the British and never came back. Perhaps he caught "the Ohio fever" and went west to settle. His neighbors stayed. For over two hundred years Parkers, Osgoods, and Hortons have lived in Blue Hill.

Jonathan Fisher, in his *Family Register of Blue Hill*, designated the people who left town but he made very incomplete statements such as, "removed from B."; "rem. to Boston." Now and then he made a fuller comment: "Died intemperate in N. Y."; "rem. deserted his wife, excluded from the Congregational Church Sept. of 1820."

R. G. F. Candage in his sketches about Blue Hill families gave little information about the town's out-goers. Typical of his information are these: "Removed to Aroostook"; "Died in Mass."; "Went to Portland and was twice married." Candage always gave specific information about sailors. He took care to name the ships on which they sailed and often wrote of shipwrecks.It is evident that Captain Candage had little interest in Blue Hill men and women who left to farm in the Midwest or mine in California or work in the mill cities of New England.

I have talked with Elizabeth Wescott and Captain Almon Gray, who are well versed in family history. I have talked with numerous friends about their ancestors. I conclude that some families were more apt to leave town than were others. The Grays, for example, have always been out-goers. From Brooksville they came to Blue Hill. From Blue Hill they went to neighboring towns and Massachusetts cities, and to the farms and forests of the West. The Grindles tended to cling to home. The Candages have not been out-goers. Recently a member of the family said to me, "We Candages like Blue Hill and we stay here."

John Roundy Snow was the first Snow to come to Blue Hill. His three sons lived in town. One of the sons, Benjamin, had six sons, five of whom stayed in Blue Hill. The sons and daughters of the five lived in Blue Hill. A few farmed, others were postmasters, R. F. D. drivers, plumbers, and carpenters. Not until the fifth generation did the Snows become out-goers. Though some of the family members have left town, in 1989 there are still Snows, Hinckleys, Osgoods, Dodges, Hortons, and Longs living on ancestral acres.

Before 1870 many men left their homes and went to sea, although most of them spent the winter months at home. Many of them came back to Blue Hill to live when they were old. R. G. F. Candage was an exception. He was born at Blue Hill Falls, educated at Blue Hill Academy, and was briefly a schoolteacher. He was certainly one of Blue Hill's most successful sailors. He started as a hand on a small fishing boat and he ended as the captain of great ships that sailed to all the ports of the world, from Honolulu to London. When he retired, he lived in Brookline, Massachusetts.

Candage was certainly Blue Hill's most versatile sailor. After his retirement, he went into business and represented his town in the Massachusetts legislature. He was one of the founders of both the Brookline, Massachusetts, and Blue Hill Historical Societies. He did research on Blue Hill history and families. He wrote verse and had two books published, *Autumn Leaves* (1901) and *More Autumn Leaves* (1903). Several of his poems deal with Blue Hill.

In 1838 the Blue Hill Light Infantry, sixty-nine soldiers and three officers, went north to take part in the so-called Aroostook War, an unpleasantness concerning the Canadian boundary. Nathan Ellis, Jr., was the captain of the company. The same year Charles Jarvis of Ellsworth led Hancock County workers to build a hundred-mile military road that went from Mattawamkeag to Houlton. When the soldiers and the workers returned home, they spread the good news of the rich Aroostook soil. In the next decade numerous people from Hancock County towns went north to farm or to cut timber.

The Mexican War had no effect on Blue Hill's population. Blue Hillers regarded the war as an attempt at "stealing bigger pens to cram with slaves." Not one volunteered to fight in the conflict, although James Candage, the brother of Captain Candage, commanded a transport that took supplies to the army.

The craze for gold drew men to California. In my childhood folks used to say, "There were fourteen Forty-niners who came from Blue Hill." I cannot name that number. But I can name five who came home: Jairus Osgood; James Long; Tyler Hinckley, who after his return drove a span of fast horses that were described by his neighbors as "bought with Tyler's gold nuggets"; John Edward Horton, who was to die in a Confederate prison; and Francis Cousins, who came home to be a successful captain and shipbuilder. Louise Frederick told me that her grandfather, Alfred Osgood, who lived at the base of the mountain, loaned money to a Blue Hiller who was California-bound. She does not know whether the loan was returned but she does know that the recipient was grateful. He sent to Mr. Osgood and his wife a stickpin, cuff links, earrings, and a brooch made from California gold.

Francis Cousins had three brothers and a sister who went to California. The brothers did well. They stayed away from mining, about which they knew nothing. They worked with ships and shipping, about which they knew a great deal. Isaiah and Nahum Wood went to California but they did not prosper. Furthermore, they were homesick. Finally they saved enough money to return home. But things had changed for them so that they felt strange, and they borrowed money from their prosperous half-brother, Giles, and went back to California.

The Civil War had a great effect on the population of Blue Hill. The soldiers who had survived the long marches, the battles, and the imprisonment in Confederate prisons rejoiced to return home. But many of them chose not to stay. Farming and fishing and going to sea no longer appealed to them. They chose to find new homes and new ways of making a living. Irving Osgood, the son of Jairus Osgood, was typical of the soldiers who sought a new start in life. When he was mustered out in 1865, he started home with his last army pay in his pocket. He stopped in Boston and spent his money on a two-week course in photography and ordered a van with a darkroom. When he got home, he bought a horse and in a few months he took to the road and went from town to town taking pictures. In a few years he settled down in Ellsworth and opened a photography shop. He trained his sons Ernest and Embert to be photographers. Embert continued the business of his father and Ernest set up shop in Berlin, New Hampshire. He trained his daughter May to be a photographer. She did her work in Laconia, New Hampshire.

After the Civil War many women and men left Blue Hill to work in cities. Some of the women probably went to Waltham to work in the watch factories. I know that five Orcutt girls went from Brooksville to Waltham. Two of Thomas Osgood's daughters went to Chicago. I wonder what drew them to a city that was so distant. Their brother Willis and a neighbor, Edward Tucker, went to Boston to learn the meatcutter's trade. Both men eventually came home. In my childhood nearly every child had a relative who worked or taught in the Boston area. My cousin Maud taught school in Medford. My great-aunt Linda was head trimmer in a Brockton hat shop. Twice a year she sent Grandmother Maddocks a box of hats that had served the trimmers as samples.

Now and again a person left town seeking better health. In the early nineteen hundreds Herbert Gray was stricken with consumption. He went to California. He was cured. He stayed.

When granite quarries and cutting sheds closed down temporarily or for good, workers left town. When the Chase Granite Company went out of business about 1915, the Italian workers, who had lived on "Peanut Row," went to Stonington and Hallowell. When the copper mines closed in the late 1890s, when the reopened mines closed at the end of World War I, most of the non-native miners went to out-of-state quarries and mines.

In the early decades of the twentieth century more Blue Hill young people went away to college. When they graduated, there was no work for them in Blue Hill. From necessity they became out-goers. Frank Maddocks was educated as a mining engineer and found work in Greensburg, Pennsylvania. Edward Everett Chase was educated as a lawyer and joined a Portland law firm. Paul Saunders was trained as a journalist and found employment in Redbank, New Jersey. Edwin Leach earned a degree in medicine and became a navy doctor. Jane Littlefield and Lois Greene trained as nurses and served in hospitals far from home. Elizabeth Wescott and Kathleen York were educated to be librarians and worked in libraries far from their native state. Robert Parker, dentist, and Malcolm Herrick, architect, were two more of the many young Blue Hillers who went away to practice their professions.

Wallace Perkins and Virginia Chase were native young people who went away to college. Wallace was born in Penobscot in 1901. His family moved to Blue Hill when he was twelve years old. The family's new home was beside the Mill Brook, not far from the home of Judge Chase. A special friendship grew up between Wallace and Virginia, the fifth Chase daughter. Their friendship continued through grammar school and the Academy and they had one year together at the University of Maine. Virginia spent the last years of her college education at the University of Minnesota, where her sister Mary Ellen taught. The two wrote to each other while Virginia was in Minnesota and while she taught in Washington County and Livermore Falls. They were married in 1927.

Virginia Chase Perkins became a college teacher and writer. Her novel *The American House* gives a fine picture of life in a Maine town at the opening of this century. Her novel *Discovery* raises questions about a woman's place in society. Her *One Crow, Two Crow* is a distinguished novel. Her short stories have been favorably compared with those of Sarah Orne Jewett.

Wallace Perkins after his graduation went to work for General Electric and spent his career with the company. His name appears on 500 GE patents. He developed the stroboscopic light that is used in the scanning device that he invented. Supermarkets now use this scanning device at their checkout stations.

For several years Wallace and Virginia Perkins owned the Augustus Osgood house at the base of Blue Hill Mountain. After she became a widow, Virginia spent years in her home village and owned a home there. Both Wallace and

Virginia were generous friends of Stevens Academy. They
were always proud that they were Blue Hillers.

Otis Ward Hinckley was another out-goer who came
home. He was a direct descendant of Joseph Wood, one of
the town's first settlers. He was the grandson of Dolly
Fisher Stevens, the daughter of Jonathan Fisher. He grew up
in the house that was built by his great-great-grandfather
Theodore Stevens. Young Hinckley had a quiet childhood
in a town where shipbuilding and shipping were declining.
He attended the Congregational Sunday school. His daughter Ethelwyn told me years later how much her father
enjoyed the Sunday school picnic held every summer. The
teacher always took the class to the same spot on the shore
of Parker's Point. The children ate their picnic on a flat rock
on the shore where they could see the blue bay, the village
half-hidden by elms, and the mountain with its twin hills.
Every year Otis Hinckley made the same resolve: "When I
grow up, I shall go away and make a fortune; I shall come
home; I shall buy the land by this shore; I shall build a house
and live here."

Otis Hinckley went to Chicago and made a fortune in the
bottling of spring water. He returned to Blue Hill and
bought the land beside the picnic shore. There he built a
house modeled after the Frank Lloyd Wright houses that he
had seen in the Chicago suburbs. Otis's house is in the
Prairie style of Wright's first houses. There is only one other
house of this style in Maine, the Albert Graves house in Ken-
nebunk.

The builder of the Otis Hinckley house was Wallace
Hinckley, the brother of Augustus Hinckley and the father
of William Hinckley. Wallace Hinckley was educated at
Carnegie Technical Institute. His best-known house is the
elaborate Italian villa that he designed and built for Mrs.

Ethelbert Nevin, the widow of the composer. Wallace Hinckley's promising career was ended by his untimely death.

Otis Hinckley enjoyed his Wright house for many summers. His daughter lived in the house until her death in 1970. Both Otis Hinckley and his daughter were generous to Blue Hill. The father's gift to Stevens Academy made possible the expansion in the early 1960s. The daughter gave to the Congregational Church the house built by her great-great-grandfather Theodore Stevens. She bought from the Fisher heirs the house built by her great-great-grandfather Fisher and gave it to the Fisher Memorial that she founded and endowed. Otis Ward Hinckley and Ethelwyn were born too late to be name-givers. They were gift-givers.

Blue Hill's out-goers took with them more than a coastal Maine accent and fondness for clams. They took with them a feeling of self-worth and the expectation of success. They

Beauty Spot, Summer Home of Mrs. Ethelbert Nevin   Bluehill Falls, Maine

Courtesy of Robert Sweetall

took with them their habits of hard work and independent thinking. Blue Hill was poorer for their leaving.

Some of the out-goers returned to their native town. Some were drawn back by the illness of parents and the inheritance of property. Others grew tired of the noise and strain of city living and returned in search of security and quiet. A few left with no expectation of staying away for good. Wherever they went, they kept with them the memory of village steeples, home bay, and blue mountain.

Esther Wood;
   a true lady —
   a true sweetheart . Sody

About the Author

ESTHER E. WOOD is a descendant of pre-1790 settlers who came to Ellsworth, Orland, Penobscot, Deer Isle, Sedgwick, Brooksville, and Blue Hill, Maine.

Miss Wood graduated from Stevens Academy in 1922 and Colby College in 1926, did graduate work at Radcliffe in 1928–29 and again in 1939–40, received a master's degree from Radcliffe in 1929 and an honorary degree from Colby in 1972.

From 1926–28 she taught at Stonington High School in Maine where she fell in love with teaching. In 1929–30 she substituted at Miss Hall's School in Pittsfield, Massachusetts. In the fall of 1930, Miss Wood went to Gorham, Maine where she taught history on the same hillside campus for forty-two years. She taught in four different institutions: the Gorham Normal School, Gorham State Teachers College, Gorham State College, and University of Maine, Portland-Gorham. She retired in the spring of 1972.

In 1952 Miss Wood sold her first written piece to *The Christian Science Monitor.* For over a decade she wrote a monthly column about her childhood at Friend's Corner for the *Monitor's* "Home Forum Page."

Miss Wood has written monthly pieces for the *New England Homestead, Down East, Maine Life, Woman's Day,* and the Maine Sunday papers. She wrote the first "The Native" piece for the *Ellsworth American* in 1968, her column for over twenty years. She has written children's stories for Sunday school papers (Presbyterian) and children's magazines.

Miss Wood has been well honored. A dormitory on the Gorham campus is named for her. In 1985 the the Blue Hill Chamber of Commerce named her "Woman of the Year." In 1987 the Maine School Superintendents Association gave her an award for "distinctive service to education in Maine." In 1989 a lecture room at George Stevens Academy in Blue Hill was named for her.

Her book ventures include *Country Fare* (New Hampshire Publishing, 1976), *Saltwater Seasons* (Down East Books, 1980), and *Hannah* (Downeast Graphics, 1982).